INTRO_____ __ __ __

BUSINESS
VALUATION
FOR MATRIMONIAL LAWYERS

INTRODUCTION TO
BUSINESS
VALUATION

FOR MATRIMONIAL LAWYERS

DAVID E. AMISS

DIVERSIFIED
PUBLISHING

ENTERPRISE, ALABAMA

INTRODUCTION TO BUSINESS VALUATION
FOR MATRIMONIAL LAWYERS
DAVID E. AMISS

Published by Diversified Publishing, Enterprise, Alabama

Editor: Clarisa Marcee
Index: Russell Santana, www.E4Editorial.com
Cover and Interior Design: Yvonne Parks, www.pearcreative.ca
Library of Congress Control Number: 2023934555

Publisher's Cataloging-in-Publication
(Provided by Cassidy Cataloguing Services, Inc.).

Names: Amiss, David E., author.

Title: Introduction to business valuation for matrimonial lawyers / David E. Amiss.

Description: [Enterprise, Alabama] : Diversified Publishing, [2023] | Includes bibliographical references and index.

Identifiers: ISBN: 978-1-958331-03-3 (paperback) | 978-1-958331-04-0 (Kindle) | 978-1-958331-05-7 (ePub)

Subjects: LCSH: Marital property--Valuation--United States. | Valuation--United States. | Divorce--Law and legislation--United States. | Marriage law--United States. | BISAC: BUSINESS & ECONOMICS / Corporate Finance / Valuation. | LAW / Family Law / Divorce & Separation. | LAW / Family Law / Marriage.

Classification: LCC: KF535.7 .A92 2023 | DDC: 346.730166--dc23

CONTENTS

Foreword 1

Introduction 3

CHAPTER 1
Definitions 7

CHAPTER 2
Introduction to Business Valuation 21

CHAPTER 3
Valuation Standards and Credentials 25

CHAPTER 4
Standards and Premises of Value 33

CHAPTER 5
Types of Engagements and Reports 55

CHAPTER 6
Company, Industry, and Economic Analysis 69

CHAPTER 7
Asset Approach 79

CHAPTER 8
Income Approach 93

CHAPTER 9
Normalization Adjustments 119

CHAPTER 10
Discount Rate and Capitalization Rate 131

CHAPTER 11
Market Approach   141

CHAPTER 12
Discounts for Lack of Control and Lack of Marketability   151

CHAPTER 13
Miscellaneous Topics   171

CHAPTER 14
Common Errors   181

Acknowledgments   189

Endnotes   191

Index   205

About the Author   217

To Anna

Outside of Christ, you are my highest aim and pursuit.

I love you!

FOREWORD

When I first started in the field of business valuation, the first book I bought was the first edition of *Valuing a Business* by Dr. Shannon Pratt, affectionately called the godfather of business valuation. It was an excellent resource, but I found it difficult to read at length, and used it mainly as a go-to resource when I encountered a valuation problem. I longed for a less lengthy book that covered the major topics, that would give me a general understanding of the basic principles and concepts of valuation (see the building blocks of valuation in the Table of Contents). That is what this book hopes to accomplish. There are many different types and sizes of businesses, but they are all valued using the same principles and methods explained in this book.

David and I have worked closely together in the field of business valuations for nine years—over 80% of that time was spent in the family law arena, valuing businesses for divorcing couples or their attorneys in North Carolina. This book is intended to help family lawyers get a basic understanding of the principles of valuation—practical and theoretical—so that they can better serve their clients. A business is often the largest asset in a marital estate, and the parties invest great trust in the expertise of their legal counsel and valuation advisors. Therefore, the attorney should be prepared and able to understand the work that the business valuator is doing. As the title implies, this book is intended mainly for the family lawyer in North Carolina who is inexperienced in business valuation. It is written in plain language in relatively short chapters, to give the novice valuation attorney a basic framework and understanding of what a business valuation report is, and what it is not. It will hopefully enable attorneys to detect problems and weaknesses in a report, so that they can question the business appraiser, and obtain a better outcome for their clients.

This book will also be a good refresher for those attorneys experienced in valuations—a quick study to get ready for a mediation or trial that involves a business that has been appraised. It may also be helpful to a business owner who is wondering how his business will be valued. It is not meant to be the only resource you need—far from it. There are many, many books written on the subject, and on the many individual sub-topics that comprise a valuation, which go into much more detail than this volume. Pratt, Hitchner, Mercer, Fishman, Trugman, Fannon, Alerding, Angell, Morris, and others are all excellent authors who have been prolific on many valuation topics.

The discipline of business valuation has evolved and changed tremendously over the last 30 years, and will undoubtedly continue to change. Many valuation issues do not have a simple black and white answer—like many legal issues, it depends. Attorneys who want to keep current in this area will need to continue to update their knowledge through reading and education.

One final word: this book is not meant to be legal advice or the final word on valuation. It is meant to be a primer or refresher on general business valuation principles and issues, to give the reader an overview of business valuation in North Carolina courts. I hope you get valuable insight from it.

— Asa H. "Hank" Crawford, CPA/ABV, CVA

INTRODUCTION

In today's world, the complexity and nuances of businesses present attorneys with many difficulties where business valuations are present. Drill down a bit further to family law, and it seemingly gets more difficult. The source of the difficulties is endless with new challenges with each case. There are entire worlds of business, management, finance, accounting, and tax. Each of these fields have their training grounds, be it the classroom or on-the-job training, or a combination of both. The task of understanding each of these is the first task for anyone using a business valuation report. Beyond that, the challenges cascade down from each of those topics and more. Basic accounting records can present difficulties, especially for those business owners employing the 'dashboard method of accounting.' Then there is the potential difficulty identifying the appropriate standard of value. Something that is quite clear to the business valuator can get less clear quickly at the intersection of state statutes and case law. Of course, the existence of 'in' and 'out' spouses adds to that difficulty. Then there are more mundane things like company-specific premium, discounts for lack of marketability, reasonable compensation that can affect the value of a company significantly. All of these factors, and many more that I did not mention, make the task of matrimonial attorneys difficult when representing their clients and fighting for their best interests and outcomes.

I am not an attorney, but from my perspective, your job is difficult—very difficult. For the attorney that must engage a business appraiser to prepare a valuation and a report, and perhaps defend it on the witness stand, the job just got a lot harder. In answering the call for those that enter that arena, a basic introduction to business valuation is essential. Above, I referenced mundane topics in valuation such as company-specific premium and discounts for lack of marketability. While those topics are commonplace, they are not easy to understand. Furthermore, can the user of the report follow the logic to affirm or question the selected figures or conclusions in a valuation report? That is why a basic understanding of business valuation concepts is essential. With that understanding, the users of the report have the ability to understand the more nuanced topics within business valuation and best support their clients. Now, there are many resources on business valuations available written by very accomplished appraisers. Most of those books, however, are written for the valuation analyst—the appraiser is the primary audience. To be clear, I am not saying that the reader of this book could not comprehend or benefit from those books. I would be the first person to tell you that having them in your library is a wise investment. So what am I saying? Business valuation for the family law attorney could be described as learning a second language. Law texts, state statutes, and treatises are your first and primary language. I might be embarrassed to tell you how many times I often have to read operating agreements, court orders, or court decisions to feel like I understand what is being communicated.

For those reasons, this book is directed at attorneys, specifically, family law attorneys. Further, the book focuses on statutes, court decisions, and practices occurring in North Carolina, though the book could be beneficial for family law attorneys practicing in other states.

This book will present, in plain English, the basic concepts of business valuation to provide a foundation, a baseline knowledge for you. For the family law attorney who is closer to law school than retirement, or has little experience with business valuations, this book could be best consumed cover to cover. For the seasoned attorney who works with business valuators often, this would be a good reference book to have in your library. For either attorney, the book can assist you in providing support as you represent your clients in difficult and complex matters.

As someone with 17 years of experience as a CPA and more than 7 years preparing valuations, I have a good perspective of the technical and practical requirements of business valuation. I have valued small companies and mid-size companies, companies recently formed and companies on the last leg of the business cycle, companies in urban and rural areas, companies with sophisticated accounting functions and those with a complete lack of accounting function, service businesses and manufacturing businesses, businesses with one or two employees and those with 100+ employees. I have had the pleasure (and to my benefit) of working with some very good family law attorneys, and alongside an experienced business valuator who is a sage. All of this allows me to understand the concepts of business valuations and be able to communicate them in an understandable manner, thus helping you to develop, or further bolster, your comprehension of business valuations.

On a more personal note, I thoroughly enjoy business valuations. I did not come to it first, starting out in tax and accounting. In college I was introduced to, and intrigued by business valuation. Tax and accounting seemed safe and logical to me, with sets of rules to follow. At the time I thought of business valuation as a lot of 'art' and less of 'science' when compared to tax and accounting. I did not realize that valuation—thanks to the work of many great practitioners like Shannon Pratt—had become much more 'scientific' and structured over time. After some time working in the tax and accounting field, I was presented with an opportunity to move towards business valuation and I am glad I did. "Love what you do, and do what you love" is a cliché for sure, but it is true, and I am grateful that I can.

Whether you have little or moderate experience with business valuations, read this book. If not cover to cover (which could be difficult), then pick a subject from the table of contents that you have wanted to understand at a basic level, or another chapter that you want to know more about, and give it a read.

CHAPTER 1

DEFINITIONS

This book will use many valuation terms throughout the chapters. Many of those instances will include definitions so that you do not have to look elsewhere. In addition to those, I have included here a comprehensive list of definitions. The terms and definitions come directly from the International Glossary of Business Valuation Terms. The definitions have been adopted by the following organizations: American Institute of Certified Public Accountants, American Society of Appraisers, Canadian Institute of Chartered Business Valuators, National Association of Certified Valuators and Analysts, and The Institute of Business Appraisers.[1]

- **Adjusted Book Value Method**—A method within the asset approach whereby all assets and liabilities (including off-balance sheet, intangible, and contingent) are adjusted to their fair market values. {NOTE: In Canada, on a going concern basis.}

- **Adjusted Net Asset Method**—*See* Adjusted Book Value Method

- **Appraisal**—*See* Valuation

- **Appraisal Approach**—*See* Valuation Approach

- **Appraisal Date**—*See* Valuation Date

- **Appraisal Method**—*See* Valuation Method

- **Appraisal Procedure**—*See* Valuation Procedure

- **Arbitrage Pricing Theory**—A multivariate model for estimating the cost of equity capital, which incorporates several systematic risk factors.

- **Asset (Asset-Based) Approach**—A general way of determining a value indication of a business, business ownership interest, or security using one or more methods based on the value of the assets net of liabilities.

- **Beta**—A measure of systematic risk of a stock; the tendency of a stock's price to correlate with changes in a specific index.

- **Blockage Discount**—An amount or percentage deducted from the current market price of a publicly traded stock to reflect the decrease in the per share value of a block of stock that is of a size that could not be sold in a reasonable period of time given normal trading volume.

- **Book Value**—*See* Net Book Value

- **Business**—*See* Business Enterprise

- **Business Enterprise**—A commercial, industrial, service, or investment entity (or a combination thereof) pursuing an economic activity.

- **Business Risk**—The degree of uncertainty of realizing expected future returns of the business resulting from factors other than financial leverage. *See* Financial Risk

- **Business Valuation**—The act or process of determining the value of a business enterprise or ownership interest therein.

- **Capital Asset Pricing Model (CAPM)**—A model in which the cost of capital for any stock or portfolio of stocks equals a risk-free rate plus a risk premium that is proportionate to the systematic risk of the stock or portfolio.

- **Capitalization**—A conversion of a single period of economic benefits into value.

- **Capitalization Factor**—Any multiple or divisor used to convert anticipated economic benefits of a single period into value.

- **Capitalization of Earnings Method**—A method within the income approach whereby economic benefits for a representative single period are converted to value through division by a capitalization rate.

- **Capitalization Rate**—Any divisor (usually expressed as a percentage) used to convert anticipated economic benefits of a single period into value.

- **Capital Structure**—The composition of the invested capital of a business enterprise, the mix of debt and equity financing.

- **Cash Flow**—Cash that is generated over a period of time by an asset, group of assets, or business enterprise. It may be used in a general sense to encompass various levels of specifically defined cash flows. When the term is used, it should be supplemented by a qualifier (for example, "discretionary" or "operating") and a specific definition in the given valuation context.

- **Common Size Statements**—Financial statements in which each line is expressed as a percentage of the total. On the balance sheet, each line item is shown as a percentage of total assets, and on the income statement, each item is expressed as a percentage of sales.

- **Control**—The power to direct the management and policies of a business enterprise.

- **Control Premium**—An amount or a percentage by which the pro rata value of a controlling interest exceeds the pro rata value of a non-controlling interest in a business enterprise, to reflect the power of control.

- **Cost Approach**—A general way of determining a value indication of an individual asset by quantifying the amount of money required to replace the future service capability of that asset.

- **Cost of Capital**—The expected rate of return that the market requires in order to attract funds to a particular investment.

- **Debt-Free**—We discourage the use of this term. *See* Invested Capital

- **Discount for Lack of Control**—An amount or percentage deducted from the pro rata share of value of 100% of an equity interest in a business to reflect the absence of some or all of the powers of control.

- **Discount for Lack of Marketability**—An amount or percentage deducted from the value of an ownership interest to reflect the relative absence of marketability.

- **Discount for Lack of Voting Rights**—An amount or percentage deducted from the per share value of a minority interest voting share to reflect the absence of voting rights.

- **Discount Rate**—A rate of return used to convert a future monetary sum into present value.

- **Discounted Cash Flow Method**—A method within the income approach whereby the present value of future expected net cash flows is calculated using a discount rate.

- **Discounted Future Earnings Method**—A method within the income approach whereby the present value of future expected economic benefits is calculated using a discount rate.

- **Economic Benefits**—Inflows such as revenues, net income, net cash flows, etc.

- **Economic Life**—The period of time over which property may generate economic benefits.

- **Effective Date**—*See* Valuation Date

- **Enterprise**—*See* Business Enterprise

- **Equity**—The owner's interest in property after deduction of all liabilities.

- **Equity Net Cash Flows**—Those cash flows available to pay out to equity holders (in the form of dividends) after funding operations of the business enterprise, making necessary capital investments, and increasing or decreasing debt financing.

- **Equity Risk Premium**—A rate of return added to a risk-free rate to reflect the additional risk of equity instruments over risk free instruments (a component of the cost of equity capital or equity discount rate).

- **Excess Earnings**—That amount of anticipated economic benefits that exceeds an appropriate rate of return on the value of a selected asset base (often net tangible assets) used to generate those anticipated economic benefits.

- **Excess Earnings Method**—A specific way of determining a value indication of a business, business ownership interest, or security determined as the sum of a) the value of the assets derived by capitalizing excess earnings and b) the value of the selected asset base. Also frequently used to value intangible assets. *See* Excess Earnings

- **Fair Market Value**—The price, expressed in terms of cash equivalents, at which property would change hands between a hypothetical willing and able buyer and a hypothetical willing and able seller, acting at arm's length in an open and unrestricted market, when neither is under compulsion to buy or sell and when both have reasonable knowledge of the relevant facts. {NOTE: In Canada, the term "price" should be replaced with the term "highest price."}

- **Fairness Opinion**—An opinion as to whether or not the consideration in a transaction is fair from a financial point of view.

- **Financial Risk**—The degree of uncertainty of realizing expected future returns of the business resulting from financial leverage. *See* Business Risk

- **Forced Liquidation Value**—Liquidation value, at which the asset or assets are sold as quickly as possible, such as at an auction.

- **Free Cash Flow**—We discourage the use of this term. *See* Net Cash Flows

- **Going Concern**—An ongoing operating business enterprise.

- **Going Concern Value**—The value of a business enterprise that is expected to continue to operate into the future. The intangible elements of Going Concern Value result from factors such as having a trained work force, an operational plant, and the necessary licenses, systems, and procedures in place.

- **Goodwill**—That intangible asset arising as a result of name, reputation, customer loyalty, location, products, and similar factors not separately identified.

- **Goodwill Value**—The value attributable to goodwill.

- **Guideline Public Company Method**—A method within the market approach whereby market multiples are derived from market prices of stocks of companies that are engaged in the same or similar lines of business, and that are actively traded on a free and open market.

- **Income (Income-Based) Approach**—A general way of determining a value indication of a business, business ownership interest, security, or intangible asset using one or more methods that convert anticipated economic benefits into a present single amount.

- **Intangible Assets**—Non-physical assets such as franchises, trademarks, patents, copyrights, goodwill, equities, mineral rights, securities and contracts (as distinguished from physical assets) that grant rights and privileges, and have value for the owner.

- **Internal Rate of Return**—A discount rate at which the present value of the future cash flows of the investment equals the cost of the investment.

- **Intrinsic Value**—The value that an investor considers, on the basis of an evaluation or available facts, to be the "true" or "real" value that will become the market value when other investors reach the same conclusion. When the term applies to options, it is the difference between the exercise price or strike price of an option and the market value of the underlying security.

- **Invested Capital**—The sum of equity and debt in a business enterprise. Debt is typically a) all interest-bearing debt or b) long-term interest-bearing debt. When the term is used, it should be supplemented by a specific definition in the given valuation context.

- **Invested Capital Net Cash Flows**—Those cash flows available to pay out to equity holders (in the form of dividends) and debt investors (in the form of principal and interest) after funding operations of the business enterprise and making necessary capital investments.

- **Investment Risk**—The degree of uncertainty as to the realization of expected returns.

- **Investment Value**—The value to a particular investor based on individual investment requirements and expectations. {NOTE: In Canada, the term used is "Value to the Owner."}

- **Key Person Discount**—An amount or percentage deducted from the value of an ownership interest to reflect the reduction in value resulting from the actual or potential loss of a key person in a business enterprise.

- **Levered Beta**—The beta reflecting a capital structure that includes debt.

- **Limited Appraisal**—The act or process of determining the value of a business, business ownership interest, security, or intangible asset with limitations in analyses, procedures, or scope.

- **Liquidity**—The ability to quickly convert property to cash or pay a liability.

- **Liquidation Value**—The net amount that would be realized if the business is terminated and the assets are sold piecemeal. Liquidation can be either "orderly" or "forced."

- **Majority Control**—The degree of control provided by a majority position.

- **Majority Interest**—An ownership interest greater than 50% of the voting interest in a business enterprise.

- **Market (Market-Based) Approach**—A general way of determining a value indication of a business, business ownership interest, security, or intangible asset by using one or more methods that compare the subject to similar businesses, business ownership interests, securities, or intangible assets that have been sold.

- **Market Capitalization of Equity**—The share price of a publicly traded stock multiplied by the number of shares outstanding.

- **Market Capitalization of Invested Capital**—The market capitalization of equity plus the market value of the debt component of invested capital.

- **Market Multiple**—The market value of a company's stock or invested capital divided by a company measure (such as economic benefits, number of customers).

- **Marketability**—The ability to quickly convert property to cash at minimal cost.

- **Marketability Discount**—*See* Discount for Lack of Marketability

- **Merger and Acquisition Method**—A method within the market approach whereby pricing multiples are derived from transactions of significant interests in companies engaged in the same or similar lines of business.

- **Mid-Year Discounting**—A convention used in the Discounted Future Earnings Method that reflects economic benefits being generated at midyear, approximating the effect of economic benefits being generated evenly throughout the year.

- **Minority Discount**—A discount for lack of control applicable to a minority interest.

- **Minority Interest**—An ownership interest less than 50% of the voting interest in a business enterprise.

- **Multiple**—The inverse of the capitalization rate.

- **Net Book Value**—With respect to a business enterprise, the difference between total assets (net of accumulated depreciation, depletion, and amortization) and total liabilities as they appear on the balance sheet (synonymous with Shareholder's Equity). With respect to a specific asset, the capitalized cost less accumulated amortization or depreciation as it appears on the books of account of the business enterprise.

- **Net Cash Flows**—When the term is used, it should be supplemented by a qualifier. *See* Equity Net Cash Flows *and* Invested Capital Net Cash Flows

- **Net Present Value**—The value, as of a specified date, of future cash inflows less all cash outflows (including the cost of investment) calculated using an appropriate discount rate.

- **Net Tangible Asset Value**—The value of the business enterprise's tangible assets (excluding excess assets and non-operating assets) minus the value of its liabilities.

- **Non-Operating Assets**—Assets not necessary to ongoing operations of the business enterprise. {NOTE: In Canada, the term used is "Redundant Assets."}

- **Normalized Earnings**—Economic benefits adjusted for nonrecurring, noneconomic, or other unusual items to eliminate anomalies and/or facilitate comparisons.

- **Normalized Financial Statements**—Financial statements adjusted for nonoperating assets and liabilities and/or for nonrecurring, noneconomic, or other unusual items to eliminate anomalies and/or facilitate comparisons.

- **Orderly Liquidation Value**—Liquidation value at which the asset or assets are sold over a reasonable period of time to maximize proceeds received.

- **Premise of Value**—An assumption regarding the most likely set of transactional circumstances that may be applicable to the subject valuation; e.g., going concern, liquidation.

- **Present Value**—The value, as of a specified date, of future economic benefits and/or proceeds from sale, calculated using an appropriate discount rate.

- **Portfolio Discount**—An amount or percentage deducted from the value of a business enterprise to reflect the fact that it owns dissimilar operations or assets that do not fit well together.

- **Price/Earnings Multiple**—The price of a share of stock divided by its earnings per share.

- **Rate of Return**—An amount of income (loss) and/or change in value realized or anticipated on an investment, expressed as a percentage of that investment.

- **Redundant Assets**—*See* Non-Operating Assets

- **Report Date**—The date conclusions are transmitted to the client.

- **Replacement Cost New**—The current cost of a similar new property having the nearest equivalent utility to the property being valued.

- **Reproduction Cost New**—The current cost of an identical new property.

- **Required Rate of Return**—The minimum rate of return acceptable by investors before they will commit money to an investment at a given level of risk.

- **Residual Value**—The value as of the end of the discrete projection period in a discounted future earnings model.

- **Return on Equity**—The amount, expressed as a percentage, earned on a company's common equity for a given period.

- **Return on Investment**—*See* Return on Invested Capital and Return on Equity

- **Return on Invested Capital**—The amount, expressed as a percentage, earned on a company's total capital for a given period.

- **Risk-Free Rate**—The rate of return available in the market on an investment free of default risk.

- **Risk Premium**—A rate of return added to a risk-free rate to reflect risk.

- **Rule of Thumb**—A mathematical formula developed from the relationship between price and certain variables based on experience, observation, hearsay, or a combination of these; usually industry specific.

- **Special Interest Purchasers**—Acquirers who believe they can enjoy post-acquisition economies of scale, synergies, or strategic advantages by combining the acquired business interest with their own.

- **Standard of Value**—The identification of the type of value being utilized in a specific engagement; e.g., fair market value, fair value, investment value.

- **Sustaining Capital Reinvestment**—The periodic capital outlay required to maintain operations at existing levels, net of the tax shield available from such outlays.

- **Systematic Risk**—The risk that is common to all risky securities and cannot be eliminated through diversification. The measure of systematic risk in stocks is the beta coefficient.

- **Tangible Assets**—Physical assets (such as cash, accounts receivable, inventory, property, plant and equipment, etc.).

- **Terminal Value**—*See* Residual Value

- **Transaction Method**—*See* Merger and Acquisition Method

- **Unlevered Beta**—The beta reflecting a capital structure without debt.

- **Unsystematic Risk**—The portion of total risk specific to an individual security that can be avoided through diversification.

- **Valuation**—The act or process of determining the value of a business, business ownership interest, security, or intangible asset.

- **Valuation Approach**—A general way of determining a value indication of a business, business ownership interest, security, or intangible asset using one or more valuation methods.

- **Valuation Date**—The specific point in time as of which the valuator's conclusion of value applies (also referred to as "Effective Date" or "Appraisal Date").

- **Valuation Method**—Within approaches, a specific way to determine value.

- **Valuation Procedure**—The act, manner, and technique of performing the steps of an appraisal method.

- **Valuation Ratio**—A fraction in which a value or price serves as the numerator and financial, operating, or physical data serve as the denominator.

- **Value to the Owner**—{NOTE: In Canada, *See* Investment Value}

- **Voting Control**—*De jure* control of a business enterprise.

- **Weighted Average Cost of Capital (WACC)**—The cost of capital (discount rate) determined by the weighted average, at market value, of the cost of all financing sources in the business enterprise's capital structure.

CHAPTER 2

INTRODUCTION TO BUSINESS VALUATION

The previous chapter provided definitions of common valuation terms. In this chapter, I will lay a basic foundation of valuation by describing business valuation at a very high level. This will allow you to refer back to this chapter as you read subsequent chapters.

The appraiser and attorney must first determine what type of engagement will be needed. Under the standards I adhere to, I can prepare a *conclusion of value* and/or a *calculation of value*. Each of those engagements can be used for valuation needs in family law contexts. The calculation of value, however, is limited, subject to being changed, and generally not a valuation that an appraiser would agree to testify to.

There are two questions that appraisers must agree upon with clients early that can drastically affect the conclusion of or calculation of value. The two questions center on determining the standard of value and premise of value. The standard of value in North Carolina family law contexts is a hybrid, borrowing from both fair market value and investment value. The premise of value can be going concern or liquidation value. Meaning, is the company going to continue operating as normal or is it being liquidated?

Appraisers will request and use a significant amount of financial and non-financial information to begin to understand the business. Additionally, they will research the economy and industry. Using all of that information, and performing a significant amount of analysis, will allow them to move towards determining the value of a business.

Business valuators utilize three approaches to determine the value of a business: the asset approach, income approach, and market approach. Within each of the approaches noted, there are various methods to determine the value of a business using that approach. For example, under the income approach, the value of a business can be determined through the Capitalized Cash Flow Method or the Discounted Cash Flow Method. I have included a simple table below including several of the common approaches and methods.

Approaches	Asset Approach	Income Approach	Market Approach
Methods	Adjusted Book Value	Capitalized Cash Flow	Guideline Company Transaction
	Liquidation Value	Discounted Cash Flow	Guideline Public Company
		Excess Cash Flow	Internal Transaction

Another major consideration in valuations are discounts. There are times when it is appropriate for an appraiser to apply a discount to reflect a diminution of value. There are two common discounts: discount for lack of control and discount for lack of marketability. First, the discount for lack of control is applied to reflect the reduced amount that a prospective buyer would pay for a minority share of a business. The inability to control management decisions, cash distributions, and other important actions leads to this discount being applied. The discount for lack of marketability is applied to reflect the inability of an interest holder to convert his ownership interest into cash in a reasonable period of time. The inability could be the result of many things, including, but not limited to, the following: restrictions on transfer of interest by the ownership documents, lack of a ready market for a privately held business interest, and length of time it may take to convert the ownership interest to cash.

After the appraiser has acquired and analyzed the financial and non-financial information, selected the appropriate valuation approach and method, and determined if discounts apply, he will then begin writing the report. There are several types of reports that can be issued. Under the valuation standards that I adhere to, I may issue a detailed report, summary report, or a calculation report.

As noted before, this chapter is a very high level outline of business valuation and the process the appraiser follows. Hopefully, it will be a helpful tool to refer back to as you read the rest of the book.

CHAPTER 3

VALUATION STANDARDS AND CREDENTIALS

The phrase "business valuation" always comes with many needed qualifiers or descriptors to help the user of a valuation understand what it is and what it is not. Case in point, sometimes a business valuation is referred to as business "evaluation." When I come across this, it is an indicator that the individual I am speaking with might not be as knowledgeable about business valuations as others. Business valuations are fascinating to me for many reasons. It is a detailed look into a business, how it is built, how it has evolved, why it is profitable, why it is risky, and much more. Put another way, a business valuation is like looking under the hood of a vehicle, and taking it apart and then putting it back together. The building metaphor is an appropriate way to understand a business valuation as to how it is prepared and the report written. As with any building project, having an appropriate or licensed builder is important, as well as knowing the building codes in order to ultimately pass inspection and receive the certificate of occupancy. In this chapter, I will discuss the basic purposes for valuations, determine who can and should be valuing a business, and finally examining the pertinent standards guiding valuators.

My first experience with business valuation came very early on in my professional career. I was working at a public accounting firm as an entry level staff accountant. One of our clients was considering selling his business and retiring. That particular client asked their CPA for help valuing their business so they could begin the process. The partner in charge of the client relationship agreed to help, and estimated the value of the business using a multiple of net equity and sales. At that moment, only a few years out of college, several questions came to my mind. How did you determine that multiple? Is this the multiple that is used for all companies in this particular industry? This particular company was very profitable, much more so than other companies in their industry—is that factored in some way? Is there a better type of multiple that should be used, for example, a multiple of gross profit? In reality, there is much more that goes into a valuation than applying a multiple pulled from industry averages. You must consider each specific company with particular client bases, vendor relationships, employee bench strength, geographic and industry constraints, and at different stages in the business' life cycle. It is my intent that this book explains the 'so much more' from this example.

So why are business valuations needed? Trying to provide a conclusive list of business valuation purposes or uses is difficult because the list is very long and constantly changing. I will spare you a long list due to my express purpose of writing to matrimonial attorneys. Depending on the purpose of a valuation, some things stay the same but other things are different on a case-by-case basis. For example, the basic premise of applying an expected rate of return to an estimated benefit stream to yield an estimated value of the business is correct. Conversely, the factors to consider in doing this are inherently different as the purpose of the valuation requires them to be different. Business valuations for gift and estate purposes must consider IRS regulations. Employee Stock Ownership Plan (ESOP) valuations must consider Department of Labor regulations and rules. Primarily in view for this book is valuations for equitable distribution, which require consideration of state statutes and case law. As will be discussed in more depth later, state statutes and case law will guide and influence many aspects of business valuation in family law matters. A few of those topics include: personal vs. enterprise goodwill, discounts for control and marketability, key person discounts, and standards of value.

So who values businesses? In short, many people value businesses. Obviously, business valuation analysts value businesses. But even within that credentialed group, there are those who do it full time and those who do it in a part-time capacity. Other people providing business valuations include, but are not limited to, CPAs, business brokers, finance professionals and educators, industry experts, real estate appraisers, and more. As with anything, there is no substitute for experience. Those individuals who are credentialed full-time valuation analysts tend to produce better business valuations and reports.

There are three primary valuation credentialing bodies for valuation analysts. They are the American Institute of Certified Public Accountants (AICPA), American Society of Appraisers (ASA), and National Association of Certified Valuators and Analysts (NACVA). In addition to issuing business valuation credentials, they also issue other relevant credentials: Certified in Financial Forensics (CFF) and Master in Financial Forensics (MAFF). The chart below summarizes the credentials available and requirements to attain those credentials.

Organization	Credential / Certification	Education	Experience	Examination
AICPA	Accredited in Business Valuation (ABV)	75 hours within 5-year period preceding application	Non-CPAs - 4,500 hours within the past 5 years CPAs - 1,500 hours within the past 5 years	Pass 2-part, 6 ½-hour, 180-question multiple-choice exam
AICPA	Certified in Financial Forensics (CFF)	75 hours within 5-year period preceding application	1,000 hours within the past 5 years in forensic accounting	Pass 2-part, 4-hour multiple-choice exam
ASA	Accredited Senior Appraiser (ASA)	4-part business valuation course	5 years full-time appraisal experience	Pass 8-hour exam, and submission of one complete business valuation report
NACVA	Certified Valuation Analyst (CVA)	5-day training program	CPA, or non-CPA with two or more years in business valuation disciplines or have prepared at least 10 valuations	Pass a 5-hour multiple-choice exam, and complete a case study of a sample valuation

Organization	Credential / Certification	Education	Experience	Examination
NACVA	Master Analyst in Financial Forensics (MAFF)	50 or more hours of training, or 5-day training program, or have participated in at least 20 forensic engagements, or 2,000 hours in forensic engagements	Holder of recognized accounting or finance credential (i.e., CPA, CVA, CFF, ASA)	Pass a 5-hour multiple-choice exam, and complete a case study of a sample valuation

All credentialed individuals preparing business valuations must adhere to business valuation standards. Each of the credentialing organizations have their own promulgated standards that valuation analysts must follow. The primary standards are Uniform Standards of Professional Appraisal Practice (USPAP) for ASA credential holders, Statements on Standards for Valuation Services (SSVS) and Statement on Standards for Consulting Services (SSCS) issued by the AICPA for ABV credential holders (as well as CPAs), and NACVA Professional Standards for CVA credential holders.

As one might expect, the standards are there to establish a uniform basis for quality valuations and reports. The standards include the following sections providing requirements on the following subjects: general and ethical requirements, scope of services, development or preparation, reporting, business valuation review, and business valuation reporting requirements. The standards are important for a variety of reasons, intended to enhance the quality of valuations and reports, and provide confidence to the preparer and to the user of the valuation report.

LITIGATION TIP:

One of the first things I do in reading a report is identify what standards the valuation required and then review these standards to make sure the report is prepared in accordance with them. If it was not prepared consistent with the respective standards, it is a major red flag. Valuation analysts should have internal quality control processes that include using checklists or other documents that serve as guideposts or checkpoints, resulting in an engagement that is prepared in accordance with the respective standards.

There are many important provisions in the standards, but two worth noting for family law attorneys in North Carolina are the jurisdictional and reporting exception. Both USPAP and SSVS include an exception to their standards that if anything prescribed in their standard differs from the requirements published by governmental, judicial, or accounting authority, they may disregard that part of the standard but all other parts will remain in full effect. The second provision worth noting is the reporting exception. VS Section 100, paragraph 50 provides a reporting exception if the valuation engagement is performed for a litigation engagement. The significance or benefit, however, might not be readily apparent. VS Section 100 has several reporting standards that, if included in the valuation report, can be used by opposing counsel to attack the report or to impeach the credibility of the valuation analyst.

I have encountered the use of the reporting exception a couple of times. One time in particular an attorney forwarded me a copy of the "valuation report" from the opposing expert. Upon opening the "report," I discovered it was a single page transmittal letter. The letter included the interest being valued, valuation date, standard of value, premise of value, purpose of valuation, and value. So, to be clear, there was a lot of useful information included on the single page but it was not a valuation report. The opposing expert was utilizing the reporting exception. The benefit for the opposing expert is that my attorney and I know only the opposing expert's value. There was no support as to how they arrived at that value. So, I do not readily know where the weak spots could be or where we could differ in judgement. Accordingly, there can be a benefit to utilizing the reporting exception.

Ultimately, some person or entity wants to know what the business is worth and she wants some confidence in the established value. In my practice as a CPA, business owners were often interested in selling and would ask me what the business was worth. To which I would say, I do not know but I can determine the value by preparing a valuation. You can imagine what some of their responses were. They would often object to paying me to prepare a valuation, insisting they knew how much it was worth themselves. Since a significant component of fair market value is the concept of a willing buyer and seller, and if they were satisfied with what someone was going to pay them, then by all means avoid the valuation and save the money. At the end of those conversations I would leave them with a question: what if the buyer would pay you more than your figure? What if you are leaving money on the proverbial table? The point is, both the buyer and the seller want some sort of confidence that the price is a 'good/fair/reasonable' number. This reality highlights the importance of education, experience, standards, and credentials needed for professionally prepared valuations and reports for equitable distribution.

In fulfilling your obligation to your client, how are you ensuring that you are getting the best outcome for them? Further, that the valuation report and conclusions will stand up in court? One way to do this is to vet the chosen expert. What are her credentials? What is her experience in the respective industry needing a valuation? What experience does she have outside of valuation that could aid her? Then, to the standards, is the report she is preparing in accordance with the standards?

In returning to our building metaphor, we have finished a brief introduction to business valuation in general, and the overall valuation process. I have answered the basic question, what is a business valuation and what goes into one? Further, answering why valuations are needed? Who prepares valuations and what are their credentials? Finally, what business valuation standards exist to guide valuation analysts in their completion of the valuation and report? The next chapter will introduce concepts that help appraisers and users of the valuation reports define "value."

CHAPTER 4

STANDARDS AND PREMISES OF VALUE

In the previous chapter we discussed the standards for valuation engagements and reports. Those help determine the parameters of each valuation engagement. The foundation for valuation that must be decided early on in the process includes determining the standard of value and the premise of value. The determination of these two elements guides much of the subsequent conversation in this book, and the procedures that will be used in performing or building a valuation.

In most instances for valuations in equitable distribution engagements in North Carolina, the general standard of value and premise of value are fair market value and going concern, respectively.

If either of these were to be different, the approaches and procedures could be different. It should also be noted that if we were discussing business valuations in equitable distributions contexts for Virginia or South Carolina, it might be different as the standard of value tends to vary state by state based on each state's statutes and case law.

In what seems like a previous life, I installed ductwork for HVAC systems. I was always quick to notice and marvel at the foundation for some unknown reason. I was drawn to the concrete block columns and walls, intricate system of sills and floor joists. Ultimately, there would be an enormous amount of weight built on top of them. Even more important were the contents or occupants above. It was absolutely necessary that the foundation be sturdy and able to hold the weight above. Likewise, the foundation of a valuation is important. What will the standard of value be? What about the premise of value? What is the level of value? The answers to each of these, like the foundation of the house, supports what is above. Further, they serve to define the term "value." The type of foundation defines what can be built upon it. The financial analysis, normalization adjustments, cost of capital, discounts, ultimate value conclusion or calculation, and more can trace their footing to the answers to these questions.

Before the valuator can answer the question "What is it worth?" or "What is the value?", he must first determine the definition of value. Different definitions of value will result in different conclusions of value.

Allow me to support that statement by introducing two concepts and six terms. The first concept is standard of value. The selection of a standard of value goes to the very core of how we define value. Depending on the selected standard of value, many other aspects discussed in this book will or will not apply. The second concept is the premise of value. Premise of value is a reflection of the company's expected future. Is it being valued on the premise that it will continue to operate into the foreseeable future, or will it cease operations and be liquidated? The selection of the premise of value will have a significant impact on the way value is defined. A list of the common standards of value and premises of value follows, along with their definition, which we will discuss in more detail later in the chapter.

STANDARD OF VALUE

- **Fair Market Value**—The price, expressed in terms of cash equivalents, at which property would change hands between a hypothetical willing and able buyer and a hypothetical willing and able seller, acting at arm's length in an open and unrestricted market, when neither is under compulsion to buy or sell and when both have reasonable knowledge of the relevant facts.[2]
- **Investment Value**—The value to a particular investor based on individual investment requirements and expectations.[3]
- **Fair Value**—The price that would be received to sell an asset or paid to transfer a liability in an orderly transaction between market participants at the measurement date.[4]
- **Intrinsic Value**—The value that an investor considers, on the basis of an evaluation or available facts, to be the "true" or "real" value that will become the market value when other investors reach the same conclusion. When the term applies to options, it is the difference between the exercise price or strike price of an option and the market value of the underlying security.[5]

PREMISE OF VALUE

- **Going Concern Value**—The value of a business enterprise that is expected to continue to operate into the future. The intangible elements of Going Concern Value result from factors such as having a trained work force, an operational plant, and the necessary licenses, systems, and procedures in place.[6]

- **Liquidation Value**—The net amount that would be realized if the business is terminated and the assets are sold piecemeal. Liquidation can be either "orderly" or "forced."[7]

To further complicate matters, there may be subtle disagreement among differing groups of valuators and users of valuation reports on the definitions of the six terms referenced above. On a simplistic level, the inherent differences are surface level. The difference in fair value and fair market value is seen in the addition of the word "market." What is this qualifier? Obvious questions likely stream to your mind. What does it mean? What market? This has led to a basic understanding that fair value is broader, conceptually, than fair market value. The narrowing from one to the other is where it gets more difficult.

STANDARDS OF VALUE

Fair market value is likely familiar due to its common use as standard of value. It is commonly used in regulatory and judicial contexts, one of those being equitable distribution. As I will express later in this chapter, elements of fair market value along with investment value are both applicable in North Carolina matrimonial litigation. There are several definitions of fair market value to consider.

- **IRS Regulations**—The fair market value is the price at which the property would change hands between a willing buyer and a willing seller, neither being under any compulsion to buy or to sell and both having reasonable knowledge of relevant facts.[8]
- **International Glossary of Business Valuation Terms**—The price, expressed in terms of cash equivalents, at which property would change hands between a hypothetical willing and able buyer and a hypothetical willing and able seller, acting at arm's

length in an open and unrestricted market, when neither is under compulsion to buy or sell and when both have reasonable knowledge of the relevant facts.[9]

It would be prudent for us to review a couple of the key words, phrases, and concepts in these definitions. First, a significant concept in fair market value is how it affects the application of discounts; specifically, discounts for lack of control and lack of marketability. We will discuss both of these in detail later but it bears referencing now. These two discounts, in theory, are intended to reflect the lesser value that a buyer would give for an interest based on certain conditions, such as not being able to control the company, or restrictions in transacting the interest in any market or lack thereof, and liquidity concerns in trying to sell an interest in a private company. Second, the standard presumes a willing or hypothetical buyer. This means that the business does not have to actually be 'for sale,' contemplated being sold, or have a specific buyer in mind. A specific buyer in mind may have particular motivations or predetermined synergies in buying the business thus influencing the price and or value. This would not be fair market value. Third, the standard presumes that neither the buyer nor the seller is acting out of compulsion. The value considered is not a "fire sale" value where the business owner is trying to harvest cash to pay off some debtor, or whatever other reason would cause a forced sale. Fourth, the standard also presumes that the transaction is at arm's length, meaning not between related parties where the price or value could be influenced up or down depending on the influenced relationship. Fifth, the standard presumes that the buyer and seller have reasonable knowledge of the relevant facts. This presumption includes, at a minimum, that facts about the company in entirety, the industry, and the economy are known. Lastly, the reference to 'cash equivalents' in the definition includes the expectation that the purchase price will be paid at the valuation date or with some combination of down payment and seller financed note at market interest rates. If the interest rate were below market rates, it would represent a discount in the purchase price.

The second primary standard of value used in North Carolina matrimonial litigation is investment value. The key differences between investment value and fair market value is the nature of the buyer. Fair market value presumes a hypothetical buyer. Investment value presumes a specific buyer. The International Glossary of Business Valuation Terms defines investment value as follows: the value to a particular investor based on individual investment requirements and expectations.[10]

When a valuator is valuing a company under the investment standard of value, she must consider what synergies exist with a particular buyer. What particular opportunities are there, likely for a limited group of buyers as opposed to the general class of buyers, to increase the market share of a new owner and grow revenue? Or to leverage what a company currently does to branch off into a new line of business. What opportunities are there to reduce costs through group purchasing, shared overhead, and more. "Investment value considers value from these perspectives of the potential sellers and buyers:

- The economic needs and abilities of the parties to the transaction
- The parties' risk aversion or tolerance
- Motivation of the parties
- Business strategies and business plans
- Synergies and relationships
- Strengths and weaknesses of the target business"[11]

The final two standards of value, fair value and intrinsic value, are not used in North Carolina matrimonial litigation. Accordingly, I will only provide a brief description and how they are different than fair market value and/or investment value. The fair value standard of value is used in some financial reporting and judicial contexts. The Financial Accounting Standards Board, a body assigned with promulgating standards for financial reporting, defines fair value as "The price that would be received to sell an asset or paid to transfer a liability in an orderly transaction between market participants at the measurement date."[12] It should be noted that where fair value is utilized for the standard of value, states often apply it in their own particular nuanced manner. This definition above appears to be similar to the definition of fair market value, but is subtly different with significant effects. So what are the differences? There is no reference to having knowledge, meaning there is no requirement to be informed about the company's industry. It is understood by most that the fair value standard does not contemplate discounts for lack of control or marketability (both discussed in detail in a subsequent chapter).

The fourth common standard of value used is intrinsic value. Webster's Dictionary defines intrinsic value as "being desirable or desired for its own sake without regard to anything else."[13] Similarly, Black's Law Dictionary defines intrinsic value as "the inherent value of a thing, without any special features that might alter its market value. The intrinsic value of a silver coin, for instance, is the value of the silver within it."[14] You likely will not find this as a standard of value in any federal or state statutes. Rather, it has been and is used in particular judicial contexts such as dissenting shareholder or family law cases. The investment and intrinsic standards of value may seem similar but indeed are different. The intrinsic standard of value relates to the underlying assets themselves. That investment standard of value relates to a particular owner's perception of the value of the assets. Finally, it should be noted that as with fair value, each individual state that uses intrinsic value as their standard of value will apply it in its own nuanced way.

Before we move on to premise of value, I want to introduce two more terms, one of which was mentioned above in a definition of standard of value, that might be helpful in conceptually understanding the different standards of value. The two terms are *value in exchange* and *value to the holder*. Understanding these two terms is conceptually straightforward—they are as they sound or appear to be. In the book, *Standards of Value: Theory and Application*, the authors define value in exchange and value to the holder as follows:

- **Value in exchange**—"The value of the business or business interest changing hands, in a real or a hypothetical sale. Accordingly, discounts, including those for lack of control and lack of marketability, are considered in order to estimate the value of the property in exchange for cash or cash equivalent."[15]

- **Value to the holder**—"The value of the property that is not being sold but, instead, is being maintained in its present form by its present owner. The property does not necessarily have to be marketable in order to be valuable … The value to the holder may be more or less than the value in exchange."[16]

As explained earlier, there are four primary standards of value: fair market value, fair value, investment value, and intrinsic value. Fair market value falls under the value in exchange premise of value. Investment and intrinsic value falls under the value to the holder premise of value. Fair value can be in both, but tends to fit more within the value to the holder premise of value. These two premises make sense when you consider a practical example.

I currently own an older pickup truck. This truck is not much to look at but is great for my family, be it going to Lowes or Home Depot, going on a camping trip, or taking off the trash after Christmas when those leftover boxes mount. Recently, I considered getting a different truck, one that could pull our camper longer distances. When I went to see what trade-in allowance the dealership would give me, I was taken aback with the low figure. I ended up not trading it in. The truck had a lot more value to me and the unique ways it was perfect for my family than in trade and future sale on the open market. This was a case where the value to the holder (my family and me) was higher than the value in exchange (the car dealership, or you!).

PREMISE OF VALUE

We began this chapter by explaining that a business valuation could be defined as answering the questions, "What is it worth" or "What is the value?" Further, we introduced two concepts that need to be determined in order to get the correct answer. The first concept was standard of value, which we have already discussed above. The second is premise of value, which at a high level we could explain as the operational capacity of the subject company to be valued. The two premises of value are *going concern value* and *liquidation value*.

The most commonly used premise of value is going concern value. So what does it mean?

Let's look at two definitions of going concerns.

- *Black's Law Dictionary*—The value of a commercial enterprise's assets or of the enterprise itself as an active business with future earnings power as opposed to the liquidation value of the business or of the assets.[17]

- International Glossary of Business Valuation Terms—The value of a business enterprise that is expected to continue to operate into the future. The intangible elements of Going Concern Value result from factors such as having a trained work force, an operational plant, and the necessary licenses, systems, and procedures in place.[18]

Essentially, valuing a business under the going concern premise of value means that the valuator presumes that the business will continue into the future.

Conversely, the liquidation premise of value is defined as follows.

- *Black's Law Dictionary*—The value of a business or of an asset when it is sold in liquidation, as opposed to being sold in the ordinary course of business.[19]
- International Glossary of Business Valuation Terms—The net amount that would be realized if the business is terminated and the assets are sold piecemeal. Liquidation can be either "orderly" or "forced."[20]

It is valuing a business with the presumption that it will not continue to generate earnings and cash flow into the future. This requires the valuator to consider the liquidation value of the company's assets and liabilities. This includes consolidation of the proceeds upon disposition of the assets less expenses to be incurred in the disposition of assets. It is nuanced even further. Shannon Pratt explained these nuanced levels in the following manner:[21]

- **Value as an assemblage of assets**—Value in place, as part of a mass assemblage of assets, but not in current use in the production of income, and not as a going concern business enterprise.

- **Value as an orderly disposition**—Value in exchange, on a piecemeal basis (not part of a mass assemblage of assets), as part of an orderly disposition; this premise contemplates that all of the assets of the business enterprise will be sold individually, and that they will enjoy normal exposure to their appropriate secondary market.

- **Value as a forced liquidation**—Value in exchange, on a piecemeal basis (not part of a mass assemblage of assets), as part of a forced liquidation; this premise contemplates that the assets of the business enterprise will be sold individually and that they will experience less than normal exposure to their appropriate secondary market.

Business valuations for gift and estate purposes have established requirements or guidance at the federal level for standard of value and premise of value. However, there is no consistent statutory guidance across the individual fifty states for matrimonial litigation. Further, some states do not even specify what standard of value is to be used in these contexts. The void in statutory guidance has left determining the standard of value and premise of value to the courts. As a result, the courts can inconsistently apply the generally understood meaning of standards of value and premise of value in the pursuit of complying with their state's general statutes. In federal tax court where there is clear guidance, business valuators can differ on what the appropriate discount for lack of control and or marketability is. What they cannot disagree on is whether or not to apply discounts—that is clearly established. For matrimonial litigation that is not the case in some state jurisdictions, it is possible for one expert to apply discounts and the opposing expert to not apply them. This could very likely produce significant differences in the ultimate value of the company being valued. For matrimonial litigation in North Carolina, some issues are clear and others remain ambiguous. Two examples are discounts and personal goodwill. The family law courts in North Carolina are clear—personal goodwill (explained in detail later) is a part of the marital estate. Conversely, the application of discounts (also explained in detail later) can be unclear.

Discounts for lack of control and lack of marketability are applicable under the value in exchange concept, but not applicable under the value to the holder concept. Remember, the value in exchange is closely associated with fair market value. That standard of value is based on what a hypothetical willing buyer would pay for the business interest. Accordingly, discounts for lack of control and marketability are applicable. Conversely, value to the holder is closely associated with investment value. That standard of value presumes a specific owner (current or prospective) and the value to that owner. Accordingly, discounts for lack of control or marketability are not applicable as the business is not changing hands, nor is it going to the open market subject to market risks. In North Carolina, where the business interest being valued is non-controlling, it is clear that discounts apply. However, where the business interest is controlling, it is unclear, based on the courts whether discounts should apply.

LITIGATION TIP:

There is a court case (*Crowder v. Crowder*), discussed later in this chapter, where discounts did apply for a controlling interest. However, there are also several cases where the courts did not allow discounts for controlling interests. Accordingly, be aware (to the extent that you can) what districts have allowed a discount for controlling interest and the appellate court case where a discount was used in a controlling setting.

The other area of business valuation directly affected by application of statutes in matrimonial litigation in North Carolina is intangible property. Intangible property can include many things but the most common is goodwill. Goodwill is understood simply as the difference in the total value of a company and the value of the tangible assets less liabilities. Therefore, the appraiser is required to estimate the value of the tangible assets and liabilities to determine if goodwill exists. Additionally, valuation engagements require the appraiser to estimate the value of a company based on the earnings potential of the company (the income approach, also to be discussed in more detail later). Oftentimes, the income approach will result in a higher value than the asset approach. The explanation of that difference is intangible value, specifically goodwill. Goodwill is an intangible asset producing value, including but not limited to: customer relationships, an able and in-place workforce, name recognition, experience, internal processes, and perhaps a key person. Goodwill can be further bifurcated into two types—personal goodwill and enterprise goodwill. Personal goodwill is an intangible asset related to the value created by a specific person resulting from his skills, relationships, expertise, etc. Enterprise goodwill is an intangible asset related to the value created by an entity, unrelated to any particular person. In North Carolina, unlike other states, it is clear that personal goodwill is part of the marital estate.

What is the significance of the two types of goodwill? Conceptually, the value in exchange concept includes only enterprise goodwill. That makes sense when you consider that the person generating the goodwill is often the seller and, therefore, the personal goodwill does not actually transfer to the buyer. Conversely, the value to the holder concept includes both enterprise and personal goodwill. This also makes sense as the assignment is to consider the value of the business to the owner, not in an exchange to a hypothetical buyer. The current owner or specific prospective owner would consider and receive the value of the enterprise goodwill *and* personal goodwill. Making a determination of value as marital or non-marital is complicated and has a direct impact on the distributive award of the marital estate.

In an attempt to clarify the topics, I have prepared a table modeled after tables in a book, *Standards of Value: Theory and Applications.*[22] This table includes the two standards of value with elements applicable to family law in North Carolina.

	Value in Exchange	Value to the Holder
Standard of Value	Fair Market Value	Investment Value
Goodwill	Enterprise	Enterprise and Personal
Discounts	Applicable	Not Applicable

So, what about matrimonial litigation in North Carolina? The statutes and cases are likely not going to refer to a premise of value often. I have included a discussion of premise of value in this chapter since it is a significant concept in business valuation and will be present in the reports you will read. The statutes and cases will, however, deal with standard of value, goodwill, and discounts. So, what do the statutes and case law state as it relates to standard of value? The pertinent Statute in North Carolina is NC GS 50-20(c), which states:

> "There shall be an equal division by using net value of marital property and net value of divisible property unless the court determines that an equal division is not equitable. If the court determines that an equal division is not equitable, the court shall divide the marital property and divisible property equitably."[23]

There are two key factors here, first, the use of "net value" in lieu of any established standard of value. What is net value? That phrase does not appear in any business valuation literature. Accordingly, there is no established definition of the phrase and standard of value from the business valuation community. At the conclusion of this chapter, I will offer a definition of net value. The lack of a direct link between net value in the North Carolina General Statutes and valuation literature potentially leaves room for ambiguity and flexibility. Further, it places a burden on the court to determine what the "net value" of a business is. The second factor mentioned is important as well and removes some of the significance from the first factor. The second factor is an allowance in the statute for the court to determine what is equitable. The court has the discretion to rule or award a distribution that is equal or unequal in determining what is equitable. Accordingly, there is no clearly defined standard of value, only the responsibility of the court to determine what values and distributions are equitable.

In addition to the statute, there are many cases in North Carolina that help to navigate these questions. There are five in particular that we will review briefly to better understand what net value is, and the functional standard of value in North Carolina equitable distribution contexts.

Hamby v. Hamby—(*143 N.C. App. 635, 2001-N.C. App.*) This is a case that went to the North Carolina Court of Appeals in June of 2001. The pertinent issue for consideration under appeal was the valuation of the husband's Nationwide Insurance business. Each of the spouses in the case hired an expert to value the business. The husband's expert valued the business at $18,950 and the wife's expert valued the business at $110,000. The primary difference in the valuations centered on the husband's relationship with Nationwide. The contracts the agents have with Nationwide preclude them from transferring or selling the 'business' or their 'book of business.' The husband's expert stated "because of the unique situation that Mr. Hamby's in, and the fact that he doesn't have control over many areas, ... you can't be sure that the future earnings will be like the past earnings." Mrs. Hamby's expert's testimony with regard to standard of value and premise of value is significant. I have included an excerpt from Mrs. Hamby's expert as it highlights an aspect of valuing businesses in North Carolina for equitable distribution:

> To begin with I valued the … Agency as a going concern. It was a going concern on the date of separation. And it's my understanding when we say we're valuing at fair market value we're trying to determine what if the entity that's being valued could have traded hands on the date of separation, date of valuation. We don't have to know there's a buyer. It's a hypothetical situation … . We know on date of separation that the sale wasn't imminent nor was it necessary. So my purpose in valuing, and I think the appropriate purpose in valuing the agency at date of separation is what is it worth to Mr. Hamby as a going concern. So I certainly agree with the definition of a going concern, is one that we do expect it is an operating entity and we expect it to continue to operate as it has been in the most recent past. So there are many businesses that I valued that might not be able to trade hands that easily … . However, there can still be a value to having a practice or agency over and above just earning a salary. [24]

The appellate court referenced the *Beightol v. Beightol* case in defining the three steps that a trial court must take in order to make a determination on equitable distribution. The steps listed are:

1. Determining which property is marital property;
2. Calculating the net value of the marital property—which is the *fair market value* less any encumbrance on the property; and
3. Distributing the property in an equitable manner.

Finally, the appellate court agreed with Mrs. Hamby's expert noting "[W]e agree with the trial court and Mr. Whitt, in that even though Mr. Hamby cannot sell it, the agency still has value as to Mr. Hamby above and beyond a salary or the net worth of the agency's fixed assets which could be sold."[25]

The appellate court's reference to the *Beightol v. Beightol* case affirms fair market value as the stated standard of value. Mrs. Hamby's expert clearly references fair market value and includes components of the definition of fair market value in his testimony. Accordingly, it is clear that the stated standard of value for the appellate court and Mrs. Hamby's expert is fair market value. But is that the functional standard of value used to determine the value of the business?

Based on two key phrases in the case, the investment value standard of value is also applicable to the functional standard in this case. One phrase by Mrs. Hamby's expert and the other by the court. Mrs. Hamby's expert stated "So my purpose in valuing, and I think the appropriate purpose in valuing agency at the date of separation is what is it worth to Mr. Hamby as a going concern."[26] Fair market value considers a hypothetical buyer, a willing buyer. This is, or can be, very different than the value to a particular person. The standard of value that considers a particular person, or the present owner, is more akin to the investment value standard of value. So while Mrs. Hamby's expert references aspects of the definition of fair market value, his value conclusion appears to be an investment value, or at the very least a combination of fair market value and investment value.

Second, the appellate court's statement, agreeing with Mrs. Hamby's expert, "that even though Mr. Hamby cannot sell it, the agency still has value as to Mr. Hamby above and beyond a salary or the net worth of the agency's fixed assets which could be sold."[27] There are several observations to be made from this single sentence that support the argument I am making with regard to the standard of value in North Carolina family law contexts. The court notes that Mr. Hamby cannot sell his agency, and instead seems to affirm that the only thing he could sell are the fixed assets (equipment, furniture, and fixtures) of the agency. Accordingly, it could be inferred that if the fair market value standard of value had been functionally used, the value of the agency would have been an asset value (total assets less total liabilities). This would have excluded the intangible value, specifically personal goodwill. The court, however, states that the value beyond the tangible assets is appropriate for consideration in equitable distribution. This is value that could not be sold or compensated for—in the words of the court, "value as to Mr. Hamby above and beyond a salary or the net worth of the agency."[28] This attribution of intangible value that could not be transferred could only be applicable under an investment value standard of value. From this case alone, the court affirms that net value includes elements of fair market value and investment value.

Poore v. Poore—*(75 N.C. App. 414, 331 S.E.2d 266, 1985 N.C. App. LEXIS 3680)* This is a case that was heard by the North Carolina Court of Appeals in 1985. The pertinent issue for our consideration here is the issue of standard of value and goodwill. The trial court found that the business had no goodwill and did not use the value of either of the experts. The appellate court noted that "The division of marital property upon divorce is to be accomplished by using the net value of the property, *i.e.*, its market value, if any, less the amount of any encumbrance serving to offset or reduce the market value."[29] The court referenced the general statutes and then offered their interpretation using their phrase "market value." But what is "market value"? Do they mean fair market value? We cannot be certain, but it appears so.

Later in their opinion, the appellate court notes that "the existence and value of goodwill is a question of fact and not of law."

This is a fairly strong statement with significant effects. The court went on to recognize personal and enterprise goodwill. They referenced the personal goodwill in connecting goodwill with the "age, health, and professional reputation of the practitioner." They referenced enterprise goodwill in relation to the "nature of the practice, the length of time the practice has been in existence, its past profits, its comparative professional success." As summarized in the table above, inclusion of personal and enterprise goodwill in the value conclusion theoretically and practically are hallmarks of the investment value standard of value. Accordingly, while the standard of value used in this case is explicitly an unrecognizable standard using common business valuation terminology, it is functionally the investment value standard. This matters because every valuation done and report written cite fair market value as the standard. If that were true, personal goodwill would be excluded from the value and marital estate.

Crowder v. Crowder—(*147 N.C. App. 677, 556 S.E. 2d 639, 2001 N.C. App.*) This case went to the North Carolina Court of Appeals in 2001. Thus far we have reviewed two court cases that point to a standard of value in North Carolina of investment value. This standard of value falls under the value to the holder concept. This concept does not include discounts for marketability or control. This makes sense because the objective is to determine the value to a particular owner (current or prospective), as opposed to in exchange. The *Crowder v. Crowder* case, however, introduced another factor to consider in understanding standard of value and discounts in North Carolina matrimonial litigation. The trial court reviewed significant factors with regard to the value of a logging business. For our purposes here, we would like to focus on the fourth factor, a 25% discount for lack of marketability. The court agreed to allow a 25% discount to the value of the company resulting from a lack of marketability or liquidity. The appellate court rejected some of the factors and reasoning, and accepted others. Included in those accepted by the appellate court was the discount for lack of marketability. In its opinion, the court noted "that competent evidence supported the remainder of the court's findings and conclusions, including its reliance on ... the use of a 25% deduction rate for lack of marketability." [30]

There are two significant reflections in the appellate court's decision. First, the applicability of a discount for lack of marketability. Second, the applicability of a discount for lack of marketability for a controlling interest. We will discuss discounts for lack of marketability, as well as their application to a controlling interest, in a subsequent chapter. However, it is worth noting that this is a very significant issue as some valuators and courts do not consider discounts for lack of marketability to be applicable to controlling interests. To be clear, the issue of discounts for marketability for a controlling interest in the *Crowder v. Crowder* case was not the primary issue for that case. What is important is what the allowance of discounts for marketability reflects. If you will recall from above, discounts for marketability logically apply under the value in exchange premise, and fair market value. Again, while not the primary issue, on appeal the court did not remove or change the discounts.

Walter v. Walter—(149 N.C. App. 723, 561 S.E.2d 571, 2002 N.C. App. LEXIS 290) This case was heard by the North Carolina Court of Appeals in 2002. There were several aspects of the case that were appealed. For the purposes of determining the standard of value and premise of value, this case (unlike many others) provides clear guidance. The appellate court explicitly states that in regards to the valuation of the medical practice, in an "equitable distribution proceeding, the trial court is to determine the net fair market value of the property based on the evidence offered by the parties."[31] This case and decision are helpful in understanding the appropriate standard of value in matrimonial litigation in North Carolina.

In consideration of the statutes and these court cases, we can say that North Carolina is a hybrid state in its determination of standard of value in matrimonial litigation, with elements of investment value and fair market value standards of value being applicable. It is further a hybrid in its inclusion of discounts applicable under the value in exchange premise of value. The inclusion of personal goodwill as marital property for equitable distribution is what ties these two different standards of values together. For North Carolina, there is no need to distinguish between personal goodwill and enterprise goodwill. Lastly, these court cases reflect the court making determinations consistent with the latitude and duty given to them in the statute to determine what is equitable. We have expanded on the table used above to include applicable case law.[32]

	Value in Exchange	Value to the Holder
Standard of Value	Fair Market Value	Investment Value
Goodwill	Enterprise	Enterprise and Personal
Discounts	Applicable	Not Applicable
Court Cases—Goodwill	N/A	Hamby v. Hamby
		Poore v. Poore
Court Cases—Discounts	Crowder v. Crowder	N/A
Court Cases—Standard of Value	Walter v. Walter	N/A

Finally, and in conclusion, I submit the following as a definition of net value, the standard of value for matrimonial litigation in North Carolina:

Net value as the standard of value in the N.C.G.S. is equal to:[33]

- the price [which is equal to an amount that includes all value (tangible and intangible) available and/or realized by the present or particular owner(s), with consideration of discounts for control and marketability, where applicable], that would change hands, in cash or cash equivalents, between a willing buyer and a willing seller, both having reasonable knowledge of relevant facts, neither being under compulsion.

Standard of value and premise of value are two topics that do not receive a lot of explicit attention in a valuation engagement. They are, however, two of the most important aspects of valuations in North Carolina family law contexts. Make a point to include these in your pre-engagement discussions and items to focus on in reviewing the engagement letter and valuation report.

This chapter's topic and contents might not garner as much attention as say discounts for lack of marketability or company-specific risk, but are a very important determination in the valuation assignment. The next chapter and subject could be described in a similar way. Determining the appropriate engagement, and report is important in delivering the best results for your client.

CHAPTER 5

TYPES OF ENGAGEMENTS AND REPORTS

In our continued march towards issuing a valuation report, it is next helpful to discuss the types of engagements and types of reports that will ultimately be issued in the engagement. There are two types of engagements and four types of reports that are allowed by VS Section 100. I am referencing VS Section 100 because it is one of the primary standards that I adhere to and a very common valuation standard. The types of engagements are valuation engagements and calculation engagements. The types of reports are detailed valuation reports, summary valuation reports, calculation reports, and oral reports. Each engagement and report type have the appropriate place and context for their use considering if the valuation is for equitable distribution, gift and estate, merger and acquisitions, or other purposes. I would be remiss if I did not note that there is some disagreement among valuation professionals from time to time on the type of engagement or report to be used. This underscores the need for valuators and attorneys in equitable distribution contexts to agree clearly in the beginning on the type of engagement and report to be used.

Albert Einstein famously said, "If I were given one hour to save the planet, I would spend 59 minutes defining the problem and one minute resolving it." It is similar to the maxim, "Think before you speak" or "Listen more than you talk." The undergirding truth in these quotes and maxims is applicable in business valuation as well. Understanding the assignment is vitally important in determining what type of engagement is appropriate as well as which report is appropriate. An appraiser preparing a valuation for equitable distribution in North Carolina must know the standard of value stated in the statutes and how the courts have handled standard of value, goodwill, and other elements of valuation. Along those lines, determining which type of engagement and report is appropriate is part of the early work that Einstein referred to.

There are two types of valuations, a *valuation engagement* and a *calculation engagement*. The valuation engagement is the standard engagement where the appraiser considers all three valuation approaches (asset, income, and market) and expresses the value of a business interest as a conclusion of value.[34] A calculation engagement is a lesser engagement, where the appraiser and client agree on which valuation approaches to apply, and the appraiser then applies limited procedures, and expresses the value of the business interest as a calculated value.[35] I will highlight the three main differences.

PRIMARY DIFFERENCES—VALUATION ENGAGEMENTS V. CALCULATION ENGAGEMENTS

First, in a valuation engagement, the analyst has to address all three valuation approaches, the asset, income, and market approaches (we will explain these in more detail in subsequent chapters). The analyst may ultimately use only one or two approaches in concluding upon her final value, but she has to at least consider them. On the other hand a calculation engagement, as prescribed by the Standards, allows the analyst to limit her focus to one or two approaches. There are some companies that, based upon their industry, make one or more of the valuation approaches ultimately not a good option in calculating a value. A couple of examples of this are as follows:

- **Asset Approach**—This approach is preferred where the Company and/or industry requires a significant investment in tangible assets. An example of this would be a trucking company where the fair market value of the assets (trucks and trailers) could be a better indicator of value.

- **Income Approach**—This approach is preferred where the Company and/or industry does not require significant tangible assets. Examples of these would be service companies, retail and distribution, and professional practices.

- **Market Approach**—This approach is preferred where the Company being valued can be reasonably compared with another company that has been sold recently or with another similar company where comparable sales data information is available. As we will discuss later, comparing one company to another requires significant analysis as companies can differ which could affect the market data used. With that said, an example of valuation where this method is preferred might be a franchise where fair market value data is readily available. Additionally, some quality medical practices often have well established market data that can be preferred.

Second, in a valuation engagement, the scope and extent of procedures cannot be expressly limited. A calculation engagement on the other hand can be limited. For similar reasons as noted above on limiting the approaches, in instances when it is reasonable to limit the procedures in calculating a value, an analyst can do so. This might not seem significant, and might ultimately not be significant. However, the significance is in the fact that the calculation engagement report will use language as required in the Standards: "A calculation engagement does not include all of the procedures required in a valuation engagement ... had a valuation engagement been performed, the results might have been different."[36] Did you catch it? The caveat that not all procedures were performed *and* that the results might have been different if they had been performed can cause problems in litigation. What likely will not be disclosed is the exact procedures that were omitted, and the amount or range that the report value could differ by in the report. That uncertainty and unknown can be acceptable in some engagements and unacceptable in others. To be clear, the valuation analyst should never agree to a certain set of procedures that will not give her a reasonable basis for a calculated result. Yet, the problem of uncertainty remains. Not many valuation analysts that are engaged in litigation and testifying would want to go to the stand with a calculation engagement. In response to an almost certain question from the opposing council, "What is your conclusion of value?" the valuator would have to respond with, "I have no conclusion as to the value, but I did perform some procedures and arrived at a calculated value." While being in this situation may make some appraisers uncomfortable it might become more common place in the future due to time and cost restraints inherent in valuations. As evidence for that, the Arizona Court of Appeals ruled in October of 2022 that a Superior Court did not err in relying on a calculation of value in a matrimonial litigation case.

Third, the results of the engagement are expressed differently. The results of the valuation engagement will be presented as "a conclusion of value" or commonly referred to and understood as their "conclusion."[37]

An example of the expression of the results is provided by VS Section 100, paragraph 69 as follows:

> We have performed a valuation engagement, as that term is defined in the Statement on Standards for Valuation Services (SSVS) of the American Institute of Certified Public Accountants, of ABC Company, LLC as of December 31, 20XX. This valuation was performed solely to assist in the matter of equitable distribution; the resulting estimate of value should not be used for any other purpose or by any other party for any purpose. This valuation engagement was conducted in accordance with SSVS. The estimate of value that results from a valuation engagement is expressed as a conclusion of value.

> Based on our analysis, as described in this valuation report, the estimate of value of ABC Company, LLC as of December 31, 20XX was $1,500,000. This conclusion is subject to the Statement of Assumptions and Limiting Conditions found in the applicable section of the valuation report and to the Valuation Analyst's Representation found in the applicable section of the valuation report. We have no obligation to update this report or our conclusion of value for information that comes to our attention after the date of this report.[38]

Conversely, the calculation engagement will express the results of procedures as merely a "calculated value." In addition, there will be a caveat that the calculation engagement did not include all of the procedures as required in a valuation engagement.[39] For both the valuation and calculation engagements, the resulting value may be expressed as a single value or a range. An example of the expression of the results is provided by VS Section 100, paragraph 77 as follows:

We have performed a *calculation engagement*, as that term is defined in the Statement on Standards for Valuation Services (SSVS) of the American Institute of Certified Public Accountants. We performed certain calculation procedures on ABC Company, LLC as of December 31, 20XX. The specific calculation procedures are detailed in paragraphs in the applicable section of our calculation report. The calculation procedures were performed solely to assist in the matter of equitable distribution, and the resulting calculation of value should not be used for any other purpose or by any other party for any purpose. This calculation engagement was conducted in accordance with the SSVS. The estimate of value that results from a calculation engagement is expressed as a calculated value.

In a calculation engagement, the valuation analyst and the client agree on the specific valuation approaches and valuation methods the valuation analyst will use and the extent of valuation procedures the valuation analyst will perform to estimate the value of the subject interest. A calculation engagement does not include all of the procedures required in a *valuation engagement*, as that term is defined in the SSVS. Had a valuation engagement been performed, the results might have been different.

Based on our calculations, as described in this report, which are based solely on the procedures agreed upon as previously referred to, the resulting calculated value of ABC Company, LLC as of December 31, 20XX was $1,500,000. This calculated value is subject to the Statement of Assumptions and limiting Conditions found in the applicable section of the calculation report and to the Valuation Analyst's Representation found in the applicable section of the calculation report. We have no obligation to update this report or our calculation of value for information that comes to our attention after the date of this report.[40]

The following table summarizes the differences in a valuation engagement and a calculation engagement.

	Valuation Engagement	Calculation Engagement
Valuation Approaches	All three required to be considered—Asset, Income, and Market	Only required approaches are those that the client and the valuator agree on. It may be one, two, or perhaps all three.
Scope and Extent of Procedures	Cannot be limited.	Limited to those that are agreed upon. The actual procedures within an individual approach (Asset, Income, or Market) may actually be the same as a valuation engagement, but not required to be so.
Result of Procedures	Expressed as a concluded value, or conclusion of value.	Expressed as a calculated value, or the results of agreed upon, or limited procedures.
Timing or Delivery	A valuation engagement typically takes a considerable amount of additional time to deliver a finished product as compared to a calculation engagement. This is a direct result of the additional procedures to be performed and the additional requirements for the report.	
Cost	A valuation engagement will cost more as well. How much more? It depends on the industry the company operates in, purpose of the valuation, accessibility to information, and much more, but at least double is a reasonable place to start.	
Applicable Situations	Equitable distribution, estate and gift, dispute engagements, ESOPs.	Mergers & Acquisitions, Equitable Distribution—mediation purposes only, Internal use
Pros & Cons	Remove the unknown or uncertainty that a calculation engagement leaves.	Time, cost

In the table above, you may have noted that equitable distribution is listed in both the conclusion of value and calculation of value columns. It is presented in that manner because that is what I have observed in family law contexts. Conclusions of value are the preferred engagement for a case that is proceeding to trial. They can also be used for mediation purposes. The primary use for a calculation of value in an equitable distribution setting is for mediation purposes.

It is possible that, in working with clients that have limited resources, a calculation engagement might be requested, for mediation purposes with the understanding that if the case were to proceed to trial, a valuation engagement would be necessary. A benefit of this is that the client might be able to get by with less cost invested in a valuation if the case settles. The obvious downside to this strategy is that there is a chance that a subsequent valuation engagement for trial might result in a different value. This is something that would cause many valuators to hesitate before agreeing to provide a calculation engagement for mediation purposes, myself included. I would almost always prefer a conclusion of value but understand it might not be worth the cost for the client.

Let us now move on to a discussion about the results of a valuator's work—the report. Statement on Standards for Valuation Services states that a report can be written or oral. The standards prescribe three types of written reports. The first two reports are for valuation engagements only—a detailed report and a summary report. The third report is for a calculation engagement. What is the difference between a detailed and summary report? A well-known business valuator described the difference as 50 pages and $5,000. The procedures performed (or development portion of the standards) do not change from a summary report to a detailed report. The conclusions reached for either report have to be supportable and, thus, the work performed to allow for that. VS Section 100 describes the detailed report as "structured to provide sufficient information to permit intended users to understand the data, reasoning, and analyses underlying the valuation analyst's conclusion of value."[41] Similarly, the Standards describe the summary report as "structured to provide an abridged version of the information that would be provided in a detailed report, and therefore, need not contain the same level of detail as a detailed report."[42] The difference is the additional pages to meet the reporting requirements prescribed in the standards. Further, the additional time and pages comes with a cost. The detailed report as noted in paragraph 51 of VS Section 100 states the report "should include" particular sections in the report. Sections 52 through 70 of VS Section 100 go on to provide more guidance as to what is in each section. The reporting requirements for the summary report conversely are included in just one paragraph of the Standard. That paragraph is exhaustive of what is required. Meaning, the valuator has to address each of those items only, no more, to be in compliance with the Standard, and addressing those items could simply require a sentence or several pages. Finally, the Standard's prescription for a calculation report is similar to that of a summary report, including what amounts to the minimum requirements for a calculation report.

There is one additional report allowable—an oral report. According to VS Section 100:

> [A}n oral report may be used in a valuation engagement or a calculation engagement. An oral report should include all information that the valuation analyst believes necessary to relate the scope, assumptions, limitations, and the results of the engagement so as to limit any misunderstandings between the analyst and the recipient of the oral report. The member should document in the working papers the substance of the oral report communicated to the client.[43]

An oral report is likely something that you have not heard about. The reason is because there is some apprehension in using them, and, thus, they are utilized less frequently than written reports. It might also be true because they are less prevalent in family law contexts. The apprehension is in part related to an uncertainty or unsettledness for the valuator in presenting something where there is no written record of what was said and the obvious concern about leaving something out that is required and would have been in a written report. I have presented oral reports for business valuations where the purpose of the valuation was to assist with a merger or acquisition. My method for providing an oral report was to schedule a Zoom meeting to enable the recording of the oral report. Prior to that scheduled meeting I would send to the client the valuation schedules that supported my conclusion or calculation of value. These schedules were not a report, but a 'work product' as I referred to them. By doing this, the client had schedules to support what I did, in addition to a sixty-to ninety-minute oral report. The oral report does everything that is required in a written report.

I believe that oral reports should receive more consideration in general, and specifically in family law contexts. First, for a case that could be settled in mediation where it is agreed that reports will not be exchanged, there is not any clear benefit to preparing the written report. The oral report alone will provide the value, and information on how the value was reached. Second, drafting a written report is time consuming and costly. If a report is not absolutely necessary, a cost-effective option might be an oral report.

There is one final topic that we should touch on prior to moving on to the next chapter—the reporting exemption provided by the Standards. Paragraph 50 of the VS Section 100 provides what is generally referred to as the litigation exemption. Here is Paragraph 50:

> A valuation performed for a matter before a court, an
> arbitrator, a mediator or other facilitator, or a matter

in a governmental or administrative proceeding, is exempt from the reporting provisions of this statement. The reporting exemption applies whether the matter proceeds to trial or settles. The exemption applies only to the reporting provisions of this statement (see paragraphs .47–.49 and .51–.78). The developmental provisions of the statement (see paragraphs .21–.46) still apply whenever the valuation analyst expresses a conclusion of value or a calculated value (Interpretation No. 1 [VS sec. 9100 par. .0 –.89]).

This means that certain provisions of VS Section 100 related to reporting do not apply to the valuator's report in matters "before a court, an arbitrator, a mediator or other facilitator, or a matter in a governmental or administrative proceeding."[44] The other provisions of the Standard must be followed in completing procedures to develop a conclusion or calculated value. What is the significance of this exemption? It allows the appraiser to omit certain elements from the report, using her discretion. Since the valuator will be subject to testimony and cross-examination, she has the ability and responsibility to determine how much or how little goes into the report. There are certain litigation settings that have their own rules regarding inclusions in the report. For North Carolina family law, the Rules of Civil Procedure control matrimonial litigation and do not include an explicit requirement for an expert to submit a written report in order to provide an opinion. Accordingly, an appraiser may provide a conclusion of value without a written report.

LITIGATION TIP:

The appraiser and attorney should consider if a written report will be used. Further, if a written report is used, decisions should be made about what to include or exclude from the report, in lieu of everything that the valuation reporting standards require in a written report. The questions should be asked: "What does the trier of fact need to see and hear to be persuaded that my conclusion is appropriate?" or "What disclosure is unnecessary, providing more liability than justification to my conclusions?"

The significance of this might appear to be overblown. Allow me to offer a story at my own expense. When I began the business valuation and litigation support portion of my career, I attended expert witness training, or "Bootcamp" as they referred to it, proctored by NACVA (National Association of Valuators and Analysts). Part of the training included a mock trial and testimony. The trainer was a business valuation and litigation support expert with 25+ years of experience who also served as the opposing counsel in the mock trial. Can you guess what he hammered me on? The report exemption, or rather the fact that I did not use it. He started and concentrated not on any schedule, number, or conclusion of my sanitized sample report. Instead, he focused on the "certifications, representations, and assumptions of the appraisers" portion of my sample report. This is a section where valuators express some of their assumptions and limitations on their expertise or work. Now to be clear, what I had in my sample report for the instructor to use in the mock trial was standard language. However, with each passing question, and hearing my answer from the perspective of a trier of fact, I instantly saw the benefits of utilizing this paragraph in the standards, as presumably did many others in the room. Here is an example of one of the representations in my report and the instructor's series of questions in the mock cross examination in response to the representation.

Paragraph from my sample report:	The financial statements and other related information supplied by ABC, Inc. or its representatives have been accepted without any verification as fully and correctly reflecting the enterprise's business conditions and operating results for the respective periods, except as specifically noted herein. We have not audited, reviewed, or compiled the financial information provided to us and, accordingly, we express no audit opinion or any other form of assurance on this information
Instructor's series of cross exam questions:	(1) Mr. Amiss, did you rely on financial information in the valuation?
	(2) Does the financial information used in any valuation, and specifically this valuation, have a significant effect on the conclusions reached?
	(3) I noticed in your written report that you accepted the financial information "without any verification," is that true?
	(4) Is it also true that if the financial information were to change your conclusion of value would change?
	(5) If the financial information is that integral to the conclusion of value, what basis do you have for a conclusion if you have not verified the financial information?

In wrapping up our discussion on types of engagements and reports, it is important to remind the reader that purpose and context of the valuation should drive the conversation. A calculation engagement should not be prepared when a valuation engagement is appropriate. With that said, there are appropriate places for calculation engagements which is why the authors of the Standard provided for it. So, in following Einstein's example, the pre-engagement and planning conversation is necessary in understanding the purpose of the assignment, users of the report, and more, in order to determine what type of engagement and report is appropriate, as well as if utilizing the litigation reporting exemption is best for the client.

Thus far, we have addressed much of the pre-engagement and planning parts of the valuation project, as well as non-financial aspects. Next, we will begin to move in the direction of focusing on the subject: company and financial data, both that of the company and the industry.

CHAPTER 6

COMPANY, INDUSTRY, AND ECONOMIC ANALYSIS

In the present chapter, we will make a shift in our focus from business valuations in general, to more specific topics. I have grouped three tasks together in this chapter as there is a common thread in them—analysis. Returning to the construction metaphor I introduced earlier, analysis of the desired home is necessary in determining what sort of support is required. This involves math, numbers, and the work of our engineering friends. Likewise, in order to complete a valuation, the analyst must first perform financial and non-financial analysis on the company, as well as review analysis on the industry and economy.

The importance of this part of the valuation assignment is underscored well with those unfortunate, and sometimes comical, stories of people answering the wrong questions. This is precisely what can happen if the company analysis of financial and non-financial data, as well as industry and economic factors, is not done well. A valuator, when asking, "What is the value?" can get the wrong answer if he interpreted the surrounding context incorrectly. A hilarious example of this comes from Adam Sandler in the movie Billy Madison when Billy was asked a question that he clearly did not understand. He gave a rambling, ridiculous answer to which the person asking the question strongly rebuked him and told him he, in fact, had not answered the question, and everyone was dumber because of his answer.

Analysis of the company, industry, and economy is important for several reasons. The most significant result of analysis well done is to understand and assess the various risks of the subject company. Risk of the company in general, risk of the company compared to others in the industry, or general risk of the industry itself. Risk of the current economic market and the effects that has on the particular company being valued must also be analyzed.

I will start with what is commonly called company analysis, containing both financial and non-financial information. Business valuation standards require the valuation analyst to perform analysis on financial and non-financial data, and to report the results of that analysis. The analyst is responsible for understanding the history (including financial and non-financial information) of the company so that he can determine an appropriate capitalization rate, growth rate, expected earnings, discounts for marketability, application of market multiples, and more.

As we dig a bit deeper into company analysis, we will split the discussion into two distinct parts, financial and non-financial, or quantitative and qualitative, respectfully. We start with the non-financial or qualitative information. This is where the analyst must ask a lot of questions to understand the business as much as possible, either based on time or the budget. Some analysts used a structured list of questions or a preferred model. Others have access to tools that generally provide data by industry and suggested questions for officers of the company to better understand the operations.

A well-known and commonly used tool is a SWOT analysis: strengths, weaknesses, opportunities, and threats. This tool provides a framework to understand and categorize internal and external factors affecting the company. Some appraisers will simply ask the client to prepare a SWOT analysis, with little guidance on what to consider. This provides the company with a blank slate to list the strengths, weaknesses, opportunities, and/or threats. This can be an effective method if you are dealing with someone who is going to sincerely engage in the process. In the absence of the needed engagement from the company and management, the valuator may present a predetermined set of topics for management to consider in the SWOT analysis. Examples of areas might include, but are not limited to, the following:

- Management team
- Employees
- Customers
- Vendors
- Capital
- Organizational systems
- Competitors
- Financial structure
- Governmental regulation
- Sales and marketing

There are a lot of questions that should be asked within each of those topics to further understand the subject company and its intersection with the industry and economy. A sample of those questions from a First Research report for the Health Supplement Stores industry classification are as follows:[45]

- What is the company's biggest competitive threat?

- How does the company promote the value of its products to budget-conscious consumers?
- How important are new products to the company?
- What type of relationship does the company have with its main suppliers?
- How does the company determine the right merchandise mix?
- What quality control procedures does the company have?
- Who is the company's typical customer?
- How does the company encourage customer loyalty?
- How important are cooperative funds from manufacturers?
- What role does the sales staff play in the company's marketing strategy?
- How have government regulations affected the company's operations?
- What trend has the company experienced in hiring?
- What are the company's staffing requirements?
- What main factors affect the company's profitability?

The answers to these questions and the results of the SWOT analysis will go a long ways towards providing a basis for the valuator to understand the business holistically, which will contribute towards future conclusions on risk and earnings projections.

We will now turn our attention to the financial or quantitative analysis portion of the discussion. This typically includes the following analysis: common size financial analysis, comparative analysis, trend analysis, ratio analysis, and comparative industry analysis. This will serve as our outline for discussing these analyses. Common-sized financial analysis includes reviewing financial data as a percentage of some base number. The predominate base numbers for the balance sheet and income statement are total assets and revenue, respectively. This exercise is insightful in that several figures on financial statements are better understood as a percentage of another figure, for example:

accounts receivable, fixed assets, inventory, long-term debt, salaries, cost of sales, and operating margin (revenue less all operating expenses). Common-sized financial analysis is especially helpful as it is paired with the next analysis, comparative analysis. Comparative financial analysis is simply the process of comparing a time period(s) of financial statement information with another. One year of financial statement data can be very impactful in the overall analysis and valuation assignment. However, to observe a trend, you need to have additional years to compare to. Five years of financial information seems to be a common period reported on by analysts. This is because five years is an appropriate number of years to include a complete business cycle for most businesses. For a company that is relatively consistent, observations and variances in particular years should become evident. Reviewing the statements in this manner will explain differences when identifying whole dollar variances, as well as identify accounts that require further analysis. Trend analysis identifies trends or patterns in financial statement information. The trends could be increasing from earlier years to more recent years, or they could be decreasing, or there may be no trends, which comes with its own implications. The valuator will also prepare a ratio analysis. This is an effective tool to recognize strengths or weaknesses in the performance of the company especially when compared to the specific company's peer group. Valuation analysis commonly utilize several ratios that are grouped into a few categories. A sampling of those ratios and explanation are included below:

	Ratio Name	Ratio Definition	Ideal result
Liquidity Ratios			
Current Ratio	Current Assets / Current Liabilities	A measure of a company's ability to pay short-term obligations or those within one year.	The higher the result the better; less than 1 indicates financial concerns

	Ratio Name	Ratio Definition	Ideal result
Quick Ratio	(Current Assets – Inventory) / Current Liabilities	A measure of a company's ability to pay short-term obligations with its most liquid assets.	Same as current ratio
Accounts Receivable Turnover	Revenue / Average (of beginning and ending balances) Value of Accounts Receivable	A measure of how efficiently a company collects its debts	A lower result indicates greater efficiency
Inventory Turnover	Cost of Goods Sold / Average Value of Inventory	Inventory turnover is a financial ratio showing how many times a company has sold and replaced inventory in a given period	A higher result indicates efficiency in managing inventory and lack of excess inventory
Leverage Ratio			
Debt to Equity	Total Liabilities / Net Worth	A measure of how the company is leveraged, or how it is financing its assets/operations	Depends on industry and stage in the life cycle of the business; a higher figure potentially reflects greater risk, and a lower figure represents using more expensive capital (equity)
Operating Ratio			
Gross Profit Margin	Gross Profit / Revenue	A measure of profitability before overhead	Depends on the industry, though a higher figure is always better

	Ratio Name	Ratio Definition	Ideal result
Operating Profit Margin	Net Income from Operations / Revenue	A measure of profitability of operations (excluding other income and expense)	Depends on the industry, though a higher figure is always better
Fixed Asset Turnover	Revenue / Average Value of Fixed Assets	An indicator of a company's ability to generate sales from fixed assets	Depends on the industry, though a higher figure is always better

Finally, the appraiser is going to take all of the aforementioned analyses and compare them against the results of other companies in the same industry. Now to be clear, no company will be an exact match. Efficiencies, or the lack thereof, will be highlighted. Perhaps that coincides with the results of the SWOT analysis. Maybe the gross profit margin and operating margins are better than the industry, which could coincide with a unique profit center or nuance in the subject company identified in the SWOT analysis. Comparing the company to the industry can also be helpful in understanding the company's risk tolerance: do they have less debt than the industry, do they carry greater amounts of cash on hand consistently? This can be helpful in considering what changes a prospective buyer would make, and the effects of those changes on profitability.

Hopefully by this point you can see that the individual non-financial and financial analyses are like pieces to a puzzle. Each piece affects another piece and is ineffective at communicating much of anything by itself. However, when put together, the picture is much clearer. At the conclusion of the financial and non-financial analysis, the valuator should have an in-depth understanding of the company, how it makes money, where it is strong or weak, where there is risk, where there is potential, and how the historical financials represent the company at the date of valuation and into the future. With a foundation for the company analysis laid, let us turn our focus to that of the industry in which the company operates.

Business valuation standards require that the valuation analyst understand "industry markets" in preparing the valuation.[46] The industry analysis is helpful and necessary in order to develop an understanding of the future of the industry and the company. Is it growing or contracting? How is the industry doing as it relates to the economy as a whole? In preparing an industry analysis, Jim Hitchner in his book, *Financial Valuation: Applications and Models* provides some good questions that should be asked:[47]

- What are the prospects for growth?
- What are the industry's dominant economic traits?
- What competitive forces are at work in the industry and how strong are they?
- What are the drivers of change in the industry and what effect will they have?
- Which companies are in the strongest/weakest competitive positions?
- What key factors will determine competitive success or failure?
- How attractive is the industry in terms of its prospects for above-average profitability?
- How large is the industry?
- Is the industry dominated by a few large companies?
- Are there many public companies in this industry?
- How much merger and acquisition activity is occurring?
- What are the barriers to entry?
- Is it a regulated industry?
- Who are the customers? Is that base growing?

Business valuation standards also require that the valuation analyst understand the "economic environment."[48] In the valuation assignment, the valuator will mostly look at past financial performance.

Equally important is the understanding of the economic environment where those past results occurred, the present economic effects, and (as best as we can project) the future economic effects. After all, people do not buy businesses for past results but rather for future earnings and cash flows. The reason we look at the past is that it *can* be a good indicator of where the business is headed in terms of earnings and cash flows. So what information do valuators consider, what questions do they ask, and how do they apply the results of these procedures?

All valuation projects will need to consider the national economy. Depending on the business and industry, there might also be a need to review the state, regional, and city economies. In addition to reviewing published data, the analyst will need to understand how the company operates in relation to the economy. When does the company flourish or struggle? What are the triggers or indicators for flourishing or struggling? If the company were engaged in commercial construction during COVID-19, and there was a societal move to working from home, that might affect the construction company. In what part of the life cycle is the company? What is the state of the economy? If the results of the company have been historically good and a good economy is necessary to produce those results, is the economy likely to continue to prosper?

The results of the economic analysis are helpful as they are paired with the industry and company analysis. The results of these three analyses will certainly affect the valuation. They will aid in selection of the appropriate capitalization rate and growth rate, which directly affects the value of the company. Additionally, the results of these procedures will give the analyst confidence on whether the historical results are an indicator of future results, or if the projected future statements of income provided by the client are reasonable in indicating future results. Lastly, the results of the work in this area should also influence the appraiser as he prepares the market approach and selects an appropriate market multiplier to apply to the subject company, resulting in a value under the market approach. Two areas ripe for error or discrepancy in a valuation are the selected capitalization rate and benefit stream expected to be received into the future. With an understanding of what goes into these analyses, you should be able to see a correlation between the analyses, capitalization rate, benefit stream, and more.

This chapter provided a bit of a transition from valuation underpinnings of standards of value, reports types to the substantive work in a valuation. We will continue that transition as we move to the next chapter as we will introduce the first of three approaches of valuing a business: the asset approach.

CHAPTER 7

ASSET APPROACH

In this chapter, I will introduce one of the three approaches to determining a value—the asset approach. The asset approach is often thought of as the "floor value" in comparison with the income and market approaches. This is because it typically reflects only the value of the tangible assets. In most businesses, there are intangible assets that have value. This value associated with intangible assets is the difference in the asset approaches and income approaches. This chapter will begin by introducing the asset approach, describing when the approach is commonly used and less commonly used, then move to the methods within the approach, and finally, introduce and explain common adjustments necessary to arrive at a value from this approach.

At my first public accounting job after graduation, I learned of a new method of accounting. I knew of generally accepted accounting principles (GAAP) and the tax basis. However, I had no clue what the "dashboard method of accounting" was. The partner I was working for at the time assigned me a tax return to prepare, and was introducing me to it. In the course of the discussion, he explained that one of the difficulties (besides the technical tax issues) would be the accounting. I was unsure what he meant. Remember, I was a new graduate and knew all about accounting. He proceeded to tell me that this client subscribed to the dashboard method of accounting. Meaning that with each bill, receipt, bank and credit card statements, etc. that the client received he would take them and throw them up on the dashboard of his car. Then when it came to "tax time," he gathered them up and brought them to our office for us to "do his accounting" in order to prepare the tax return. Now as you can probably imagine, that was a difficult task. We had to take all of his "stuff" and produce a balance sheet, complete with assets, liabilities, and equities. There was always the possibility of omissions, but we did the best we could with what we had.

INTRODUCTION

In the asset approach, the analyst is responsible for valuing each asset and liability of the company, then subtracting the total liabilities from the total assets to arrive at net asset value. In most cases, the valuation analyst will have to make adjustments to the business' historical balance sheets to reflect the agreed upon standard and premise of value. While that might seem simple in theory, its application can be very difficult. The completion of this approach can be made difficult by many factors, including the soundness of a company's accounting system, tangible assets that can be difficult to value (especially when the valuation budget is limited), and unrecorded assets and liabilities. Later in this chapter we will introduce many of the balance sheet accounts and account types that the valuation analyst will encounter. We will also discuss the common adjustments required to reflect the agreed upon standard and premise of value.

The asset approach is commonly used in asset-intensive companies (i.e., trucking companies), manufacturing companies, and holding companies. In these companies, the majority of a company's value is tied to the estimated fair market value of the tangible assets less liabilities, and there typically is not a significant intangible or goodwill component. Holding companies are businesses that are created with the primary purpose of holding assets and where minimal assets have been deployed in the production of income (income and return on investment are low). Other companies where the asset approach would be used would be inefficient or poorly operated companies. So while they do not have significant fixed assets, they do not have much value due to poor management, being early or late in the life of the business, or various other reasons. An example of this could be an automotive repair shop that opened in July and is to be valued in December. If it was started from scratch, it likely has not had the ability to generate a customer base and benefit from the start-up costs. If the business was valued in later years, it could have a value from the income approach that exceeded the asset approach.

The asset approach is seldom used in non-asset-intensive companies, or in minority interest valuations. Businesses that are non-asset-intensive include service businesses, construction companies that do not require significant fixed assets, and physician practices. These businesses derive their primary value from intangible assets including goodwill and non-compete agreements. For business valuations of a minority interest in a company, the asset approach is generally not applicable. The reason for this is that if the owner of a minority interest does not have the power or authority to cause the sale or liquidation of the assets, then the interest holder could never receive the value from disposition of the assets until the business is sold or terminated.

ASSET METHODS—ADJUSTED BOOK VALUE AND LIQUIDATION VALUE

The adjusted book value method is the method predominantly used in the asset approach. What is the adjusted book value method? In order to answer that question, I should first provide a brief explanation of what book value is. Book value is the equity, or total assets, less total liabilities, of the company being valued. These figures are found on the balance sheet of a company's financial statements and reflect actual historical cost of assets when they were acquired. The balance sheet is prepared one of three ways: internally generated by the management of the company, taken from the tax return of the company, or the financial statements prepared by an independent CPA. Accordingly, the adjusted book value method is the process of making adjustments to the book value to reflect the fair market value of the total assets and liabilities.

The liquidation method is another way to value a business under the asset approach. This method requires the analyst to consider what the assets, less liabilities, would be worth, not as an ongoing enterprise or going concern, but if the business was ending. Within this method, there are two considerations: is the liquidation forced or is it orderly? This decision could have a significant impact on the ultimate value of the business. If the liquidation is forced, it is likely that the disposition of assets will produce a smaller cash return than if the assets are sold in an orderly disposition. The decision depends on the overall health of the business and its operations.

ASSET ADJUSTMENTS

Now with these two methods of valuing a business under the asset approach introduced, let us turn our attention to the asset adjustments that we referenced above.

Cash—Cash typically does not require an adjustment because the balance reported on the bank statement less checks issued and un-cleared is fair market value. All accounting software includes a bank reconciliation function, which will result in fair market value. In the event that the business being valued is not using an accounting software, the valuation analysts would need to cash the bank statement(s) as a starting point and then inquire with management about un-cleared checks for any potential adjustments. There are many places where difficulties can arise in the asset approach but this typically is not one.

Accounts receivable—Accounts receivable balances commonly require adjustments for two reasons: first, the basis of financial statement reporting, and second, uncollectible accounts. The primary basis of accounting observed is cash basis (sometimes referred to as tax basis) and GAAP (Generally Accepted Accounting Principles). Financial statements prepared on a GAAP basis will include cash transactions and accruals that reflect assets and or liabilities. Financial statements prepared on the cash basis will omit accounts receivable, accounts payable, and other accruals. Additionally, the internal revenue code allows for businesses to report their income, expenses, and balance sheet on both the cash basis and accrual basis, whichever the business owner chooses. Many smaller businesses choose to utilize the cash basis for income taxes because it is simpler. Accordingly, many of these businesses use their tax basis, cash in most instances, as their method for recording transactions.

Businesses that prepare their financial statements on the cash basis or tax basis (which is likely cash basis) will have underreported assets and revenue. That fact makes the need for adjustments obvious. The valuation analyst needs to record the accounts receivable on the date of valuation balance sheet. If the past historical income statements reflect revenue on the cash basis, they too might require an adjustment to make total revenues accurate. A case could be made if revenue and accounts receivable from the oldest period to the most recent period are relatively the same that no income statement adjustment is warranted. However, if there is a trend in revenue, accounts receivable, and profitability, an adjustment to revenue for each year should be considered. The reason is that different historical years are weighted differently when there is a trend in revenue and/or profitability. Accordingly, to not adjust revenue in each year would result in an incorrect projection of future profits where the projection is based on a weighted average calculated off prior years' profits and revenues. This would have a direct effect on the value of the company. This will be discussed more in the chapter addressing income statement normalization adjustments.

The second common reason for adjustments to accounts receivable is collectability. When adding accounts receivable to the balance sheet (or if it is already recorded), the valuation analyst must consider what, if any, of the balance is uncollectible. More often than not, a portion of a business' accounts receivable is not collectible. There may be specific balances that are questionable, or a history of not collecting all of the accounts receivable. Common examples of this are physician practices.

An example of a business where an adjustment was necessary due to both unrecorded accounts receivable and uncollectible receivables is included on the next page in Figure 7.1. In this example the business was a physician's practice. I was provided with the annual charges and collections in the historical period. As you can see, there is a significant difference in accounts receivable and collectible accounts receivable. In this example, I recorded the net amount that was actually collected. If that data is not available for the most recent year, the valuator will have to use her judgement to determine an estimated collections figure based on available company and industry data. Lastly, since this company experienced significant growth in charges and collections, I adjusted revenue for each of the five historical years to reflect revenue on the accrual basis. This conversion required me to remove from revenue the accounts receivable balance from the end of the prior year as they were earned in a prior period. Next, the accounts receivable balance from the end of the present year is added to revenue as they were earned in the current period.

Figure 7.1 - Sample Adjustment for Accounts Receivable					
	Year Ended - December 31,				
	20XX	20X1	20X2	20X3	20X4
Total Charges and Collections					
Charges	3,736,202	3,256,263	3,109,080	3,381,888	2,877,822
Collections	2,129,635	1,823,507	1,803,266	1,826,220	1,496,467
Collection Percentage	57%	56%	58%	54%	52%
Balance Sheet Adjustment					
Unadjusted accounts receivable	-				
Adjustment to record accounts receivable at 12/31/21	2,129,635				
Adjusted accounts receivable balance	2,129,635				
Income Statement Adjustment					
Unadjusted revenue total	1,554,109	1,790,539	1,104,405	1,868,105	1,318,421
Prior year accounts receivable	(1,823,507)	(1,803,266)	(1,826,220)	(1,496,467)	(1,406,679)
Current year accounts receivable	2,129,635	1,823,507	1,803,266	1,826,220	1,496,467
Adjusted revenue total	1,860,237	1,810,780	1,081,452	2,197,857	1,408,209

Inventory—Inventory frequently has to be adjusted in business valuations to reflect a fair market value, for three primary reasons. The first two are similar to accounts receivable, and the third relates to the method of accounting for inventory. For businesses that do not utilize GAAP or who use a cash/tax basis of accounting, inventory is not required to be recorded. Accordingly, the analyst must determine the correct amount of inventory, and will need help from the company since the analyst will not be an expert at valuing inventory. The analyst will have to evaluate it for reasonableness though. One final note: most businesses, even if they do not have significant product inventory, will have some level of supplies inventory that should be considered unless clearly immaterial. A second reason for adjusting inventory is consideration of inventory obsolescence. Put another way, how much of the recorded inventory is worth its stated or recorded cost? Or, over time have portions of it become obsolete? The last common reason is related to LIFO (Last in, first out) and FIFO (First in, first out). These terms reflect how a company records its inventory. For valuation purposes, FIFO is a better representation of fair market value as the goods most recently purchased will remain on the balance sheet along with their related cost, which will approximate market value.

LITIGATION TIP:

Site visits can be a valuable tool for the analysts in adjusting inventory or identifying unrecorded inventory. This is one of the many reasons that site visits should be considered by the analyst.

Investments—Many small businesses that are valued do not have investments on their balance sheet. If a business does have investments, they need to be adjusted to fair market value. For companies that utilize the GAAP basis of accounting, they will likely already be at FMV. However, the other asset recognition method that is common is for investments to be recorded at "cost," which is initial cash outlay (and subsequent investments, if applicable) to acquire the investment, with no adjustment or consideration for income and or loss, or for changes in fair market value since acquisition. The adjustment required to reflect fair market value is relatively easy for marketable securities, since market value for these investments are readily available on various stock exchanges. What can be more challenging is if the investment is in anything other than marketable securities. For instance, an LLC interest holding real estate, or a minority interest in another operating company. So what can the analyst do to adjust the assets to fair market value? Ideally, management can assist in getting a value from the investment company itself. Perhaps, a valuation of the company that is invested in can be performed to determine the value. However, budget constraints can make this difficult.

Land and Buildings—Unlike accounts receivable and accounts payable that are often not recorded on the books, land and buildings are almost always recorded. The primary consideration here is to consider whether the net book value (cost less accumulated depreciation) reflects fair market value. Rarely do they since the building cost is being depreciated, while the FMV of the building may be appreciating over time. The basis for the adjustment ideally comes from a real estate appraisal. In the event one is not available, the appraiser may consider local county tax assessed value, but should do so cautiously.

Equipment and Furniture—These accounts will require an adjustment similar to land and buildings. In many cases these assets will not have any significant net book value (cost less accumulated depreciation). This is primarily due to the fact that many businesses record depreciation on the tax basis. This includes methods of accelerated depreciation that reduce the net book value of the asset far below fair market value, or even to zero. Accordingly, the balance has to be adjusted to fair market value. The source of the adjustment should come from an equipment appraiser. In the event that it is not available, management should provide an estimate to be reviewed for reasonableness by the appraiser.

Leasehold Improvements—Leasehold improvements reflect the improvements to the real property that the business is renting. The manner in which the business records the cost recovery can vary and is sometimes impacted by tax accelerated depreciation. When this is the case, the fair market value will almost certainly exceed the net book value, requiring an adjustment. Additionally, the analyst needs to consider the lease terms and expectations before trying to adjust the net book value. In the event that company's lease will end soon and might have to relocate to another location, the benefits from the leasehold improvements will not be fully recognized. In that example, the analyst might need to consider adjusting the net book value of the leasehold improvements to zero.

Intangible Assets—This is one of the more difficult areas in the asset approach. Most businesses that operate at a profit have intangible value. It is typically referred to as goodwill, though it is likely not all goodwill. The primary way to determine what the intangible value is by subtracting the asset approach value from the income approach value.

Additionally, some businesses will have "goodwill" on their balance sheet. This is probably the result of a prior business combination where assets of another business were acquired. In valuations of small businesses this asset is very difficult to value, and will likely require an adjustment as well. Ideally, the adjustment would be based on the work of an appraiser who has experience valuing this particular type of intangible asset. If a separate appraisal of the intangible is not available the valuation analyst might have to seek outside assistance.

Shareholder Loans—Shareholder loans are another difficult area that the analyst must carefully review. "Shareholder loans" can refer to *shareholder loan receivables or shareholder loan payables*. Every business is different with various circumstances and reasons for having these assets/ liabilities. The following is a brief introduction of them, why they occur, and the valuation adjustment considerations:

- **Shareholder Loan Receivable**—Three common reasons for these loans include advances to related companies of the shareholder, paying expenses that are personal in nature for the benefit of the shareholder, and distributions/compensation that the company does not want to record as compensation to avoid paying payroll taxes. The valuation analyst is responsible for reviewing these balances, their historical activity, and any available promissory note instruments. If collection of these amounts in a reasonable time frame is in doubt, or if it appears that it will never be repaid, the analyst should consider reducing the balance or removing it all together.

- **Shareholder Loan Payable**—Two common reasons for these loans are advances from related companies of the shareholder and advances from the shareholder that are functionally capital. The valuation analyst, similar to shareholder loan receivable balances, should review these liabilities to determine if they are legitimate. More often than not for small businesses, the shareholder loan payables will never be paid back in full. In that case, they are functionally contributions of equity by the owner and should be adjusted to reflect that.

Accounts Payable—Accounts payable will require an adjustment similar to accounts receivable. First, the payables will have to be recorded if the company being valued uses the cash basis of accounting. Second, the valuation analyst will need to review the accounts payable listing to determine if there is any doubt that all of the payables will actually be paid.

Other Current Liabilities—Much like their current asset counterparts, current liabilities often require an adjustment. The reason for the adjustment is similar—cash basis financial statements will not record these liabilities. Examples of these liabilities include accrued payroll, accrued interest payable on debt obligations, and accrued distributions/dividends.

Debt—The two primary considerations in reviewing loans, excluding lines of credit, is determining that the recorded current portion of long-term debt is correct and determining if the debt is necessary or required for operations. Ultimately, the cumulative balance will not change, thus the value from the asset approach will not change no matter how the balances are divided between current and non-current. Where it is valuable though is in the analysis of the company, consideration of excess cash/working capital (to be discussed later), and potentially the market approach (discussed later).

Deferred Tax Asset/Liability—Deferred tax assets and liabilities are the result of timing or permanent differences in recognition of income and expenses from the GAAP basis of accounting to the tax basis of accounting. The valuation analyst is responsible for reviewing the recorded balance(s) to determine if deferred tax benefits or obligations will actually be recognized in the near future. If the appraiser determines that it would not be recognized soon, she may consider reducing the recorded asset or liability. Consider an example of a manufacturing company that generated net operating losses (NOL) of $3.5 million in the first year of operations, and another $1 million of losses in the second year. The tax law allows these losses to be deducted in the future to offset income. If, however, the income projections for the company indicated that it would be more than five years to produce enough income to use up these NOLs, then the analyst may reduce the deferred tax asset. The reason behind the adjustment is that the benefit of the $4.5 million in losses would be utilized so far in the future that the present value of the losses should be discounted.

Adjustments—Income Tax Effects—After all of the adjustments have been made to the balance sheet the valuator needs to consider one final adjustment—to reflect the income tax effects of the adjustments made. All of the adjustments to assets and liabilities ultimately have an effect on income and expenses. Consider an example: $100 of accounts receivable corresponds with $100 of income. That income will be taxed (let us assume a 21% tax rate for this example), resulting in a cash benefit of $79. The same is true for expenses. Accounts payable of $100 corresponds with $100 of expense. Although after recognizing a deduction of $21 for income taxes, the cash outlay is $79. This is an over simplification, but hopefully is helpful in summarizing the adjustment. The appraiser will add up all adjustments to current assets, less all adjustments to current liabilities, then apply a reasonable income rate to record the income tax liability associated with the balance sheet adjustments.

I have included an example below in Figure 7.2 of a balance sheet with several of the adjustments we discussed above.

Figure 7.2 - Sample Balance Sheet Adjustments			
	Unadjusted Year Ended December 31, 20XX	Adjustments	Adjusted Year Ended December 31, 20XX
Assets:			
Current Assets			
Cash	125,000	-	125,000
Accounts Receivable	-	725,000	725,000
Other Current Assets	35,000	-	35,000
Total Current Assets	160,000	725,000	885,000
Fixed Assets			
Land & Buildings	3,250,000	(75,000)	3,175,000
Vehicles	225,000	(25,000)	200,000
Equipment & Furniture	650,000	(250,000)	400,000
Leasehold Improvements	350,000	-	350,000
Accumulated Depreciation	(1,500,000)	-	(1,500,000)
Total Fixed Assets	2,975,000	(350,000)	2,625,000
Non-Current Assets			
Loan to Shareholder	125,000	-	125,000
Other Non-Current Assets	50,000	-	50,000
Total Non-Current Assets	175,000	-	175,000
Total Assets	3,310,000	375,000	3,685,000
Liabilities & Equity:			
Liabilities			
Current Liabilities			
Accounts Payable	-	250,000	250,000
Line of Credit	200,000	-	200,000
Current Portion of LT Debt	125,000	-	125,000
Payroll Liabilities	25,000	50,000	75,000
Other Current Liabilities	75,000	-	75,000
Income Tax Effects	-	89,250	89,250
Total Current Liabilities	425,000	389,250	814,250
Long-Term (LT) Debt			
LT Debt - Equipment Note	475,000	-	475,000
LT Debt - Building Note	1,350,000	-	1,350,000
LT Debt - Building Upfits	275,000	-	275,000
LT Debt - Vehicles	125,000	-	125,000
Total Long-Term Debt	2,225,000	-	2,225,000
Total Liabilities	2,650,000	389,250	3,039,250
Equity			
Common Stock	10,000	-	10,000
Retained Earnings	650,000	(14,250)	635,750
Total Equity	660,000	(14,250)	645,750
Total Liabilities and Equity	3,310,000	375,000	3,685,000

Once all of the adjustments have been made, the total adjusted assets, less total adjusted liabilities, equals the value of the company based on the asset approach. It should be noted that this is the value prior to any discounts, which will be discussed later. The value of the company in the example on the previous page, based on the asset approach, would be $645,750.

The asset approach can be thought of as the easiest approach. Hopefully, we have shown in this chapter some of the potential complexities of the asset approach and the specific procedures and adjustments contained within. My hope is that in understanding the potential complexities, you will be better equipped to critically review the balance sheet, adjustments, and resulting asset approach value.

I introduced the first of three approaches (in no particular order) to value a business. Out of the three, the asset approach probably garners the least amount of attention and focus in many valuations. The next approach is likely the opposite. The income approach is the focal point in many valuations. That approach is seeking to determine the value of a business based on the earnings capacity of the business. It is a fascinating approach, filled with potential pitfalls and full of implications for the conclusion of value.

CHAPTER 8

INCOME APPROACH

In this chapter I will introduce a second approach to valuing a business—the income approach. This approach is likely the most widely known and utilized approach. The income approach is often a better approach than the asset approach because the asset approach typically does not reflect the value from the intangible assets of a business. The income approach is often a better approach than the market approach because small and medium size businesses are so very unique. While the market approach can provide a basis for conclusion of value or a good sanity check, it obviously fails to reflect the attributes of the specific company being valued. Things such as management team, maturity of business, access to capital, and much more can explain appropriate differences in values derived from the income and market approaches.

For all of these reasons, I have dedicated a significant portion of this book to the income approach. I have decided to separate the income approach and related aspects of completing this approach into three chapters. In this chapter, I will introduce the income approach including methods and the overall process of developing a value through this approach. The two additional chapters will discuss the application of discounts and capitalization rate, and normalization adjustments required.

My son came to me one day expressing a desire to create a business. He did not say, "Dad, I want to start a business," but that was the essence of the conversation and the request. He wanted to buy a sheep. He had exhibited sheep several times at local and state livestock shows. I remembered with fondness the experience of caring for the animals, preparing to show the animals, and learning many good habits along the way. Not only did he want to show the sheep, he wanted to own several sheep, and make a business out of it.

My mind was immediately flooded with thoughts, questions, and objections. The appraiser and accountant in me could not resist, it is how I am trained, and how I am wired. What ensued was a conversation with him about the potential costs and revenues from his sheep enterprise. He was very confident it would work. To his credit, he put time and thought into explaining to me that it could "make money." My wife and I were left with a decision: invest in this enterprise or not. In order to do that, we had to consider the potential cash inflows and expenses, the net income that he said it could provide. Were his estimates accurate? Did they need to be adjusted? In addition to these considerations, there was something else we had to consider. What was the risk that his enterprise would produce the income or cash with the stated investment? You probably have similar examples, perhaps a lemonade stand or a lawn mowing business for the neighborhood. This simple and memorable experience is a decent example of what is happening when a valuation analyst prepares an income approach to value a business.

INTRODUCTION

The fountain head of the theory undergirding the income approach in valuation is to consider the business as an income-producing investment. What amount of benefit, return, or cash will a potential investor receive in the future, sufficient to induce them to invest now. A more detailed explanation of this concept is that:

> [t]he value of an asset is the present value of its expected returns. Specifically, you expect an asset to provide a stream of returns during the period of time you own it. To convert this estimated stream of returns to a value for the security, you must discount this stream at your required rate of return. This process of valuation requires estimates of (1) the stream of expected returns and (2) the required rate of return on the investment.[49]

> An investment requires a commitment of dollars that the investor currently holds, in exchange for an expectation that the investor will receive some greater amount of dollars at some point in the future. This is one of the most basic premises of business valuation: Value is forward-looking. This "forward-looking" premise is basic to all investment decisions and business valuations … . The income approach to business valuation embraces this forward-looking premise by calculating value based on the assumption that the value of an ownership interest is equal to the sum of the present values of the expected future benefits of owning that interest.[50]

In an effort to summarize and simplify these explanations, the value of a company derived through the income approach is reflected in a fraction:

$$\text{Value} = \frac{\text{Benefits}}{\text{Rate of Return}}$$

Admittedly, the above fraction is overly simplified in that there are many additional elements within the numerator and denominator. My intent here, however, is not to dazzle you with algebraic formulas but to concisely explain what is happening in the income approach. The quotient, or the result in division is the value, or perhaps more appropriately stated as the present value. The numerator reflects the future benefit stream of the company. As noted in the explanations above, the expected benefit stream must be forward looking. In other words, what stream of benefits will be received in the future? This makes sense when we remember that investors are not buying what the company did in the past, instead they are buying or investing in a company for what it will produce after the date of valuation.

The denominator reflects the associated risk or required rate of return connected with the expected benefits represented in the numerator. Stated another way, it "reflects the opportunity cost, or the 'cost of capital.' [I]t is the rate of return that investors require to draw them to a particular investment rather than an alternative investment."[51] The total (reflected as a percentage) reflects elements of rate of return, expected inflation, and risk. Rate of return is required to be considered to compensate the investor for the use of the money. The investor is "letting" the company use his capital as opposed to deploying it elsewhere. What return is required for that to happen? Rate of return is intended to reflect that. Expected inflation has to be considered because a dollar earned and returned to the investor tomorrow is not worth the same as a dollar today based upon the time value of money principle. If the computed benefits earned in the future (represented in the numerator) is $1 million, the present value of those benefits is something less than $1 million. Finally, the denominator considers the risk with a particular investment and the expected benefit stream from the investment.[52] I have included a table below to reflect how changes in "benefits" and "rate of return" change the value. Hopefully, by this point, it is clearer than mud.

Numerator (Benefit Stream)						
Increase	in	Benefits	=	Increase	in	Value
Decrease	in	Benefits	=	Decrease	in	Value
Denominator (Rate of Return)						
Decrease	in	Return	=	Increase	in	Value
Increase	in	Return	=	Decrease	in	Value

One final comment before moving on: it should be noted that the benefits and return conclusions should be in concert with one another. As we will note later in this chapter and in subsequent chapters, there is some flexibility and variability as to how appraisers will determine the benefits and return. One example of that is the notion of pre-tax versus after-tax. The benefits represented in the numerator can include tax effects or not. Same for the return represented in the denominator. The point is, they cannot be mixed. If the benefits figure is after-tax, the rate of return figure needs to be after-tax as well. This is an area where errors sometimes occur.

With a foundation laid for understanding the income approach, we will turn our attention to a brief discussion on the common applications of the income approach as well as some advantages and disadvantages of the approach.

ADVANTAGES AND DISADVANTAGES OF THE INCOME APPROACH

The income approach is useful for valuations of businesses in most industries. It might not ultimately be used as the final value, but it has a significant contribution. The income approach is especially useful in companies that are services business, professional practices, manufacturing, construction, and more. Some of the advantages include: the usefulness of the results in making financial decisions, relative straightforward nature of how it is computed, and helpfulness in determining intangible value of a company.

Some of the disadvantages come in determining the numerator and denominator. The valuator cannot know what the actual benefits received in the future will be. Thankfully, there are a lot of tools that can be employed resulting in a credible number. Additionally, what is the best percentage to use for the rate of return? Keep in mind that whatever figure is used should appropriately reflect elements of rate of return, inflation, and risk. Any one of those three would be difficult in and of itself. Couple them together and it is an ever more difficult task. As with the benefits, there are a lot of tools available to the analyst to reduce the uncertainty inherent in the rate of return. Later in the book is a chapter on common errors in valuations. It probably does not come as a shock to you that benefit streams and rate of returns are included in that chapter. Subtle differences here or there within the numerator and denominator can be the source of significant errors and differences in the concluded value of a company when two different valuators are engaged. A nationally known valuator, Jim Hitchner, presented a course at a valuation conference entitled "How to Detect and Attack a Rigged Valuation." In that presentation, he listed drivers for errors within the income approach. They were: discount rate, growth rate(s), and cash flows.[53] The first two drivers directly relate to rate of return in our equation. The last driver is benefit stream. This point emphasizes the need to exercise discretion in selecting the business valuator to use in your cases. Selecting an analyst who will not be compromised, and will let the value be what the value is, obviously is paramount. Additionally, selecting an analyst that can articulate in report and testimony the appropriateness of their selections for benefits and return is equally important.

The income approach consists of several ways or methods of determining a value of a business. In this manner, it is similar to the asset approach having the adjusted net asset method and the liquidation method. These methods include the following:

- Discounted cash flow method, commonly referred to as "DCF"
- Capitalized cash flow method, also known as the capitalization of earnings method
- Excess cash flow method, also known as the excess earnings method

Each of these methods can be used within the income approach to produce a value of a business. As you might expect, careful consideration should be taken by the analyst in determining which method is best to use. In some valuations, more than one method may be appropriate and available. A few examples of necessary considerations for the analyst in determining which method to use include the following:

- Purpose and users of the valuation
- Industry that the business operates in
- Management involvement in preparation of financial data
- State of the economy and industry

Each of the methods uses the formula we introduced above, though the excess earnings method adds a twist that we will discuss later. The two components of the formula introduced above were benefits and rate of return. Return is commonly referred to as the discount rate or even the capitalization rate. It is complicated and central to an income approach done well. To that end I have devoted an entire chapter of the book to covering discount rates, capitalization rates, build-up methods, weighted average cost of capital and more. For now we will focus on the numerator, or benefit stream of the formula. Once we have introduced that we can move on to a brief discussion of the three methods.

BENEFIT STREAM

Defining and determining the benefit stream is essential to deriving a credible value. The foundation for determining the benefit stream is the company's financial statements, primarily the profit and loss statement. But they are just that, the foundation and starting point. The valuation analyst has to make adjustments to those financial statements, commonly referred to as normalization adjustments. If you recall, the benefit stream that we are interested in is a future benefit stream. While the historical financial statements are important, to the extent that they do not represent income or expense in the future they need to be adjusted. Furthermore, based upon our understanding of standards of value, specifically for fair market value, our goal is what a hypothetical buyer would expect to receive as income. Businesses often have expenses that have no business purpose, for example, expenditures that are for the personal benefit of the owner. Consideration must be made for all of these reasons and more. The result of these adjustments will be a re-stated income statement. Due to the significance of the topic, I have set aside an in-depth handling of normalization adjustments in the next chapter.

Once the normalization adjustments have been made, the valuation analyst then has to decide what type of benefit he will use to define future benefits. To put it another way, the analyst has to decide between using earnings (or net income) or cash flows to estimate future benefits of the company. Earnings can be defined as the revenue less cost of sales, general and administrative costs, and other income and expenses. It is also known as net income. It can be a good indicator of benefits earned in the past and what is possible in the future. It is used primarily in connection with capitalization methods as opposed to discounting methods. Using earnings as an indicator of future benefits can be argued to be more straightforward than using cash flows, which requires several specific assumptions about future balance sheet activity that is difficult to know. Additionally, where management is less sophisticated, the financial records are not robust, and earnings in the historical period are steady, the earnings method is not only an acceptable approach, but perhaps the wise one. Lastly, in smaller companies the earnings can sometimes approximate cash flows.[54] In Figure 8.1, I have included a single year profit and loss statement showing the unadjusted totals with normalization adjustments resulting in the adjusted profit and loss statement. In this example the figure to be considered to reflect the possible future benefit stream is the adjusted net income amount of $250,995.

Figure 8.1 - Sample Single Year Adjusted Profit and Loss Statement with Normalization Adjustments			
	Unadjusted December 31, 2020	Normalization Adjustments	Adjusted December 31, 2020
Revenues	7,589,584	-	7,589,584
Cost of Good Sold	(5,692,188)	-	(5,692,188)
Gross Profit	1,897,396	-	1,897,396
Operating Expenses	(1,487,953)	(171,432)	(1,659,385)
Net Operating Income	409,443	(171,432)	238,011
Other Income	75,485	(62,501)	12,984
Net Income	484,928	(233,933)	250,995

Using cash flows to estimate the benefit stream is a reasonable and commonly used method. Cash flows can be used in either capitalization methods or discounting methods. In using cash flows, the analyst is tasked with converting earnings (or net income) into cash flows. The theory behind using cash flows is that it is a better indicator of benefits available to the investor in the form of dividends and distributions. In championing the use of cash flows, a well-known valuator had this to say: "[m]any profitable companies go out of business, but it is rare that we see a business with solid cash flow go under."[55] We have included below a relatively basic cash flow model and will discuss it further below.[56]

Figure 8.2 - Cash Flow Model
Begin with: Normalized net income
Add: Normalized Non-cash expenses
Less: Anticipated capital expeditures
Add or Subtract the Net: Working capital adjustment
Add or Subtract the Net: Debt issuance or payments
End with: Net cash flow

The first thing you should notice is that the model begins where the earnings model ended, with normalized net income. From there, a series of adjustments are made to convert the earnings figure to a cash flow figure. A brief discussion of each of these follows below.

- **Non-cash Expenses**—Expenses included in net income that are non-cash expenses such as depreciation and amortization should be added back to net income.

- **Anticipated Capital Expenditures**—Depreciation and amortization, absent tax incentives to accelerate and inflate the amounts, are intended to represent the normal cost recovery of capital assets. Those assets that will provide income-making power and ability beyond one year, and those items that are not purchased routinely like supplies. In the previous step, the non-cash expenses were removed, such as depreciation and amortization. A prudent business should elect to invest annually in machinery, equipment, and more in order to continue and/ or grow operations. Accordingly, with the non-cash items of depreciation removed, the valuation analyst must subtract some figure that approximates the annual capital expenditure outlay.

- **Working Capital Adjustment**—Working capital is defined as the total current assets less the total current liabilities. "Current" simply is a designation that the assets and liabilities will be received, recognized, or paid within the next year. Another way to define working capital is the cash needed to support the business in the next twelve months. Cash, accounts receivable, inventory, accounts payable, and current portion of long-term debt are a few examples of current assets and liabilities. The valuation analyst has to consider what amount of working capital is necessary and reasonable moving forward. Considerations include current net working capital, what would be necessary moving forward at a constant level of activity, and what would be required to grow the business.

- **Debt Issuance and Payments**—Lastly, the valuation analyst has to consider what changes to long-term debt will occur. This includes the possibility of new debt being issued, perhaps connected with the second bullet point of capital expenditures, and with the certainty of principal repayments of long-term debt. It comes as no surprise that in a cash flow model, debt issuance and re-payments can have a significant effect on the cash flow available to the business and ultimately to investors.

We started our trek through the income approach with the historical income statements. Next, we discussed briefly normalization adjustments (more in the next chapter). Following that, we introduced the need to determine or define the type of benefit stream—earnings (or net income) and cash flows. Before we can move on to a discussion of the common methods used in the income approach, we need to discuss what earnings or cash flows are considered for determining the numerator in our formula. The example of normalization adjustments above includes a single period. However, the valuation analyst routinely needs to consider multiple years in the historical period to develop a foundation for determining the future benefits to be received.[57] Let us dive into a discussion of how we use the historical data and then we will move on to a discussion of the methods.

There are five commonly understood ways that business valuators can use the historical data to estimate future earnings, though some of these are used more frequently than others. The list below comes from a text authored by Jim Hitchner, but it is commonly known among valuation analysts.[58] None of the methods below are overly complex; to the contrary, the difficulty arises in trying to choose the best method when more than one might be appropriate.

- **Current Earnings Method**—This method uses the most recent period of financial data to estimate future earnings capacity. The benefit or advantage of this method is that it is easy to apply and understand. The use of this method requires the analyst to believe that the future years will be similar to this most recent year. The downside of this method is that it is very limited and does not contain an entire business cycle. This discussion leads into the next few methods.

- **Simple Average Method**—This method uses a simple average of the historical financial data to estimate future earnings capacity. The method uses multiple years in the attempt to represent a full business cycle. Many analysts prefer to use five years believing that amount of time represents a full business cycle. Perfect or without flaws? Certainly not, but over five years it is believed the business will likely experience normal and natural fluctuations in supply-chain issues, staffing problems, negative and positive economic effects, normal product demand fluctuation. However, there are situations when less years is appropriate and five years is not appropriate. The following are some reasons that business valuators may use different numbers of periods:

o **New(er) Company**—Perhaps the company is younger than five years. Obviously, in that instance, the analyst will not use five.

o **Change in Product**—If there has been a significant change, or addition, in product or service offering, consideration may need to be given to changing the number of years used to reflect only the new product or offering.

o **Addition of Capacity**—If the company significantly increased its capacity to produce a product, it would be prudent to use the years that include the additional capacity and perhaps only the additional capacity. This makes sense when you consider a simple example. A manufacturing company that is 15 years old and until three years ago had one factory. Then three years ago it added another factory, significantly adding capacity. As a result of that, almost everything on the profit and loss statement (revenue, cost of sales, and overhead) is different than the last three years. As such, it is likely that the analyst would forego using the years with just one factory, instead using the most recent three years. In essence, the historical period for this example represents two different companies with two different values.

o **Outlier**—A business, industry or economy can experience from time to time a year that is outside of the normal business cycle, which might not reoccur in the foreseeable future. A great example of this is Covid-19. If a business had a year or two affected by Covid-19, and has fully recuperated, omitting that year(s) from the computation of the future benefit stream might be appropriate.

We have included an example below to illustrate the application of this method.

Figure 8.3 - Benefit Stream Selection - Simple Average					
	2020	2019	2018	2017	2016
Net Income / Cash Flows	789,000	715,000	725,000	595,000	475,000
Weight	1	1	1	1	1
Subtotal	789,000	715,000	725,000	595,000	475,000
Total of years					3,299,000
Total weight					5
Simple average of net income / cash flows					659,800

- **Weighted Average Method**—The primary difference here is instead of weighting each historical period the same, the valuator places different emphasis on specific years. A simple average is appropriate when there is no discernable trend in the financial statements. When there is a discernable trend (with emphasis on profitability), the business valuator should consider weighting individual years differently. This is commonly done when there is the appearance of increasing or decreasing profitability. In this case you may see weighting of "5, 4, 3, 2, 1" used or the inverse. The intent is to recognize trends while at the same time considering the "business cycle" we referred to above. The potential downside to this method, and the simple average method, is that they potentially are "conservative" in projecting the earnings or cash flow capacity of a company. If indeed there is any positive trend, slight or significant, in earnings or cash flows it could be argued that the selected earnings or cash flows amount is a "floor" amount in a sense. Yet, the methods are still effective at producing conclusions of value, commonly used by valuators, and respected by triers of fact. We have included an example below to illustrate the application of this method.

Figure 8.4 - Benefit Stream Selection - Weighted Average					
	2020	2019	2018	2017	2016
Net Income / Cash Flows	789,000	715,000	725,000	595,000	475,000
Weight	5	4	3	2	1
Subtotal	3,945,000	2,860,000	2,175,000	1,190,000	475,000
Total of years					10,645,000
Total weight					15
Weighted average of net income / cash flows					709,667

In addition to the above example, we included an additional example to reflect how the selected net income or cash flow figure changes if one of the years is excluded as an outlier.

Figure 8.5 - Benefit Stream Selection - Weighted Average, excluded 2016					
	2020	2019	2018	2017	2016
Net Income / Cash Flows	789,000	715,000	725,000	595,000	475,000
Weight	4	3	2	1	-
Subtotal	3,156,000	2,145,000	1,450,000	595,000	-
Total of years					7,346,000
Total weight					10
Weighted average of net income / cash flows					734,600

- **Trend Line-Static Method**—The trend line-static method is based on the least squares formula. This formula and method produce a trend line that lessens the influence of any single year of data on the overall selected earnings or cash flow amount. Additionally, it places a greater emphasis on the more recent years in the analysis. A steady trend (up or down) of results and expected growth is necessary to apply this method. We have included an example below to illustrate the application of this method. You will note that not only does this method produce the highest figure among the methods introduced thus far, but actually greater than any one year based on this particular fact pattern.[59] This is because this method assumes that the upward trend will continue to the first future year.

Figure 8.6 - Benefit Stream Selection - Trend Line-Static					
	2020	2019	2018	2017	2016
Net Income / Cash Flows	789,000	715,000	725,000	595,000	475,000
Weight	5	4	3	2	1
Result of application of method					809,400

- **Formal Projection Method**—This method is completely different from the four prior methods discussed. The primary difference is the shift from using historical data to using projected or forecasted data to arrive at the expected future benefits from operations. In this method, the valuation analyst utilizes future cash flow or earnings projections to determine the benefits of the business. These projections tend to be three to five years in length, but exceptions can, and often do apply. The length of the projection is associated with how far into the future projections can be reasonably relied on. Some businesses, if they have sophistication and knowledge/experience in the industry, are able to project the revenue, cost of sales, and indirect expenses for a few years into the future. On the other hand, knowing the profitability of a business beyond five years in the future is difficult. The source of projections can vary depending on the business and what advisors the business has. The valuation analyst must closely review the projections for reasonableness, and discuss questions about the projected figures with management and/or business owners. This review includes consideration of the following: comparing the projections to the historical financials, comparing the income projections to future projected balance sheets, how the projections fit with the company analysis and interviews of management, capacity within the company to hit the projection, and economic and industry opportunities or constraints.

INCOME APPROACH METHODS

Thus far in this chapter we have introduced the income approach. This approach requires the valuation analyst to look at the business as an investment. The value of the company as defined by the income approach is related to the future benefits provided by the company and a corresponding required rate of return. The formula I introduced was: value is equal to benefits divided by rate of return. The equation is intended to simplify and assist in understanding; however, it is difficult to apply. Entire books have been written on the numerator and denominator of that formula. Now that the foundation has been laid, I would like to draw these individual concepts to a conclusion by discussing the main methods for determining the value of a company through the income approach. The first two that we will cover—capitalized cash flow / earnings method and discounted cash flow method—are by far the most commonly used methods. But the last method (excess earnings method) is included because you might run across it from time to time, and you should have a basic understanding of it.

CAPITALIZED CASH FLOW (EARNINGS) METHOD

The first method is referred to as the capitalized cash flow method (or capitalized earnings method). Understanding this method will provide a foundation for understanding the discounted cash flow method. First, I will provide definitions for terms that we will be using in the ensuing discussion, some of which have already been used. The definitions come from the International Glossary of Business Valuation Terms.[60]

- **Capitalization of Earnings Method**—A method within the income approach whereby economic benefits for a representative single period are converted to [a present] value through division by a capitalization rate.

- **Capitalization**—A conversion of a single period of economic benefits into [a present] value.
- **Capitalization Factor**—Any multiple or divisor used to convert anticipated economic benefits of a single period into [a present] value.
- **Capitalization Rate**—Any divisor (usually expressed as a percentage) used to convert anticipated economic benefits of a single period into [a present] value.
- **Discount Rate**—A rate of return used to convert a future monetary sum into a present value.

The formula for the capitalized cash flow or earnings method is expressed as follows:[61]

$$PV = \frac{E_1 \text{ or } NCF_1}{k - g}$$

Where:

PV	=	Present value
E_1	=	Expected benefits expressed as earnings or net income one year immediately into the future from the valuation date
NCF_1	=	Expected benefits expressed as net cash flows one year immediately into the future from the valuation date
k	=	Discount rate or cost of capital
g	=	Expected annual growth rate of E_1 or NCF_1 into perpetuity

This should look familiar based on what we introduced earlier. Present value using the capitalized cash flows (or earnings) model includes dividing the benefit stream (expressed as a selected net earnings or cash flows amount) by a rate of return (expressed as a capitalization rate). You will likely note that there is a "$_1$" beside the 'E' and 'NCF.' Once the valuation analyst has selected his benefit stream amount, he will apply the expected growth rate for the year immediately following the date of valuation to arrive at the selected benefit amount to capitalize. That amount is divided by a capitalization rate. The capitalization rate is simply the discount rate less the expected long-term growth rate into perpetuity. We will discuss in more detail the discount rate, capitalization rate, and growth rates in a subsequent chapter. I do want to mention here that the growth rate is the expected growth rate long-term *into perpetuity,* not what it will average over the next five years. I have included a table on the next page to illustrate the application of this formula and approach. Included in the table are four different scenarios corresponding to the different methods valuators can use to determine the expected future benefit stream. Each of these methods began with the same earnings or cash flow data for years 2016 through 2020. Notice how different the results are when extrapolated out through this approach. The trend line-static method results in a 23% higher value than the simple average method. Hopefully, this displays the significant differences that can result based on assumptions about the past performance of the business, the future capacity, the industry and economic drivers, and other considerations. Lastly, note that the total has been expressed as a rounded figure. Valuators typically do this, or disclose a range of values. We do this because while valuation theory and application are supported by studies and data, it is not an exact science. To say the value of the business is exactly $3,691,314 is unnecessary. Instead, the business is worth $3,691,000 or perhaps $3,700,000.

Figure 8.7 - Summary of Values by Method				
	Simple Average	Weighted Average	Weighted Average Excluding 2016	Trend Line Static
Net Income / Cash Flows	659,800	709,667	734,600	809,400
1 Year Growth rate	3.5%	3.5%	3.5%	3.5%
Selected benefit to capitalize	682,893	734,505	760,311	837,729
Discount rate	21.5%	21.5%	21.5%	21.5%
Long-term growth rate	-3.0%	-3.0%	-3.0%	-3.0%
Capitalization rate	18.5%	18.5%	18.5%	18.5%
Selected benefit to capitalize	682,893	734,505	760,311	837,729
Capitalization rate	18.5%	18.5%	18.5%	18.5%
Value - Income approach	3,691,314	3,970,297	4,109,789	4,528,265
Value - Income approach, rounded	3,691,000	3,970,000	4,110,000	4,528,000

DISCOUNTED CASH FLOW METHOD

Now, let us dive into the second method, the discounted cash flow method or DCF as it is commonly referred to. A working definition of the DCF is "a method within the income approach whereby the present value of future expected net cash flows is calculated using a discount rate."[62] The DCF is similar to the previous model in that it has an element of capitalization to it, as well as the basic concept of value being equal to benefits divided by rate of return. It is different in that it is premised on estimating specific future earnings or cash flows for several future periods and discounting them back to the present value; instead of taking a selected single-period earnings amount and capitalizing it forward. The formula for the DCF method is as follows:[63]

$$PV = \sum_{i=1}^{n} \frac{E_i}{(1+k)^i}$$

Where

PV   =   Present value

Σ = Sum of

n = The last period for which economic income is expected; n may equal infinity if the economic income is expected to continue into perpetuity

E_i = Expected future economic income in the ith period in the future (paid at the end of the period)

k = Discount rate or cost of capital

i = The period (usually stated as a number of years) in the future over which the prospective economic income is expected to be received

The formula and definitions above might be confusing—it is for most the first time they see it. Allow me to offer up an expanded formula to assist in understanding.[64]

	Present Value of NCFs during Projected Period(s)					Present Value of the Terminal Period

$$PV = \frac{NCF_1}{(1+k)^1} + \frac{NCF_2}{(1+k)^2} + \frac{NCF_3}{(1+k)^3} + \dots + \frac{NCFn \times (1+g)}{(k-g)} \frac{}{(1+k)^n}$$

So, let us walk through the formula to try and gain a greater understanding of what is happening here. I will start by drawing your attention to the two segments in the formula above, present value of NCFs during the projected period(s) and present value of the terminal period. Before we move on, we should note that "NCF" means net cash flows. Typically in the DCF method, net cash flows from operations are the primary focus instead of earnings. There are two segments that are combined in the DCF to arrive at present value (PV). The first segment includes estimating the net cash flows for a certain number of individual periods subsequent to the date of valuation. In the example above, you can see three specific periods of NCFs identified, NCF_1, NCF_2, and NCF_3. We also left a "placeholder" in the example for additional periods. The number of periods used in the projected period will differ in each valuation but three to five years is common in valuations. Ultimately, analysts will use however many periods they feel confident in, or until they feel like the cash flows will be constant moving forward. Projecting specific cash flows much past five years could be considered too speculative. The NCF from each period then has to be discounted back to the present value. That is what the denominator in the fraction above is accomplishing. Then all of the discounted cash flows from the specific periods are added together to get the present value from that segment, which is then added to the present value from the next segment to arrive at the concluded value from the income approach.[65]

The second segment, present value of the terminal period, includes both capitalization and discounting. Thus far in the DCF method we have considered the present value for specific periods into the future, three in the example above. What about the present value of the net cash flows for periods beyond these years? The terminal value addresses that. Terminal value (also known as the residual value) is "the value as of the end of the discrete projection period in a discounted future earnings model."[66] How does the valuator determine the terminal value? This is accomplished by determining what the expected growth rate is into perpetuity beyond the last projected period. Apply that growth rate to the last NCF from the final projected period and capitalize it into the future. It is in that way that the DCF uses elements from the capitalization model. However, the valuation analyst has one additional step to take. He must then discount those capitalized cash flows back to the present value. I have provided an example in Figure 8.8 to illustrate the application of this method.

Figure 8.8 - Summary of Discounted Cash Flow Method					
	Projected Periods				**Terminal**
	Period 1	**Period 2**	**Period 3**	**Period 4**	**Period**
Net cash flows at beginning of period	65,000	74,750	88,953	104,074	113,441
Growth rate for period	15%	19%	17%	9%	5%
Net cash flows at end of period	74,750	88,953	104,074	113,441	119,113
Discount rate	23%	23%	23%	23%	23%
Present value factor	0.813	0.661	0.537	0.437	0.437
Present value of net cash flows of period	60,772	58,798	55,888	49,574	

Summary of present value of net cash flows		Terminal Period Computations	
Projected Period 1	60,772	Discount rate	23%
Projected Period 2	58,798	Less: Long-term growth rate	-5%
Projected Period 3	55,888	Capitalization rate	18%
Projected Period 4	49,574		
Terminal period	289,180	Capitalized cash flows	661,740
Present value of cash flows	514,212	Present values of net cash flows	289,180

In this example, there is a specific growth rate for the first four years of 15%, 19%, 17%, and 9%, followed by an assumed long-term growth rate of 5% into perpetuity. For each period of the projection you see how the cash flows are determined and then discounted back to the present value. Finally, you can see the terminal cash flows of $119,113 capitalized into the future resulting in a value of $661,740 at the end of year 5, and then discounted back to the present value of $289,180. Adding the individual projected periods and the terminal value results in a present value of $514,212 from the discounted cash flow method. Now, let us turn our attention to the last method we will discuss, the excess cash flow method.

EXCESS CASH FLOW METHOD

The excess cash flow method is also known as the excess earnings method. The excess cash flow method was introduced to split the value of business between net tangible assets and intangible assets. This method is not used as frequently as the other two methods. IRS Revenue Ruling 68-609 includes this comment in its discussion of the method, "[t]he 'formula approach' may be used in determining the fair market value of intangible assets of a business only if there is no better basis available for making the determination."[67] The IRS's comments are more significant in gift and estate tax valuations than in matrimonial litigation in North Carolina. However, the comments do reveal concern for the method that is observable in its use, or lack thereof. There are specific contexts where it may be a valuable method to utilize. One example is in matrimonial litigation where personal goodwill is a non-marital asset. In that context, valuators will often use this method to separate the value associated with tangible assets and enterprise goodwill, from that of personal goodwill to be excluded from the marital estate. This, of course, is not applicable in North Carolina based on case law that indicates both personal and enterprise goodwill are a part of the marital estate. Accordingly, I will not give this method the attention that we did for the other two methods. But I do want to offer a brief introduction of the method. Two important definitions to cover first are as follows:

- **Excess Earnings**—"That amount of anticipated economic benefits that exceeds an appropriate rate of return on the value of a selected asset base (often net tangible assets) used to generate those anticipated economic benefits."[68]
- **Excess Earnings Method**—"A specific way of determining a value indication of a business, business ownership interest, or security determined as the sum of a) the value of the assets derived by capitalizing excess earnings and b) the value of the selected asset base. Also frequently used to value intangible assets."[69]

In explaining this method, I thought it would be best to offer a simple example and then walk through the example.

Figure 8.9 - Summary of Excess Cash Flow Method		
Expected benefit stream - cash flows or earnings		275,000
Long-term growth rate		4.0%
Selected benefit to capitalize		286,000
Tangible net assets	450,000	
Rate of return for tangible assets	20.0%	
Return on tangible net assets	90,000	(90,000)
Excess earnings		196,000
Capitalization rate		18.5%
Intangible value		1,059,459
Tangible net assets		450,000
Total entity value		1,509,459
Total entity value, rounded		1,509,000

The example above begins with a benefit stream, much like the prior two methods, and then applies a long-term growth rate to reflect the benefit stream at the end of the following year. At that point the selected benefit is ready to be capitalized. However, this is where this method is different from other methods. The example above then lists the tangible net assets—the total tangible assets less related liabilities. A rate of return is assigned to those assets resulting in $90,000. This figure represents the return or benefits produced by tangible assets. Once this amount is subtracted from the total benefits of $286,000, the intangible benefits alone (excess earnings) remain totaling $196,000. This amount is then capitalized to arrive at the intangible value of the business. That figure is added to the value of the net tangible assets resulting in a total value of the business of $1,509,000.[70]

Several years ago, as I mentioned above, I attended NACVA's (National Association of Certified Valuators and Analysts) Expert Witness boot camp. This is a training session where business valuators gather to receive training on providing expert testimony in a litigation context. It was at this training that a conversation took place that is now etched in my memory. During one of the breaks, a conversation ensued about the use of the discounted cash flow method (DCF) and capitalized cash flow method. One particular person recounted rather emphatically his recent experience. He was involved in litigation and had used the DCF, while the opposing expert used the capitalized cash flow method. The judge sided with the opposing expert. I am unsure of the specifics of the case and why the judge ruled the way she did. What I am certain of is that the issue for the person telling the story was that the judge would even consider the capitalized cash flow method. For him, the DCF was the far superior method. He was right that the DCF is a very good method, but he was wrong that it is the only method or that capitalization is an inferior method. The reality is that the DCF and capitalization methods done well can and should produce the same result.

The purpose of this chapter was to introduce the income approach. There are two additional subjects that deserve attention that are of great significance to an income approach: normalization adjustments and rate of return. I touched on these two subjects in this chapter, but because of their significance, decided to give them their own chapter. Accordingly, with the foundation laid, please continue through the next two chapters to develop a fuller understanding of the income approach.

CHAPTER 9

NORMALIZATION ADJUSTMENTS

This chapter discusses normalization adjustments, which were introduced at a cursory level in the prior chapter. Normalization adjustments are a significant part of the income approach. These adjustments are made to the historic financial statements of the business, and are necessary for a proper application of the income approach. In this chapter, I will explain what normalization adjustments are, introduce the types of adjustments, and finally offer examples of common adjustments.

The significance of this chapter and the next chapter cannot be overstated. Earlier in the book, I introduced building a house as a metaphor for a business valuation. To return to that metaphor, an error made in judgement as it relates to normalization adjustments, could be akin to getting the engineering wrong on the building plans. What seems okay, right or appropriate in the moment will obviously be wrong at some point thereafter. The income approach is trying to determine the present value of future benefits. It is not just one year of benefits, or two. Rather, it is the present value of all future years' benefits. Accordingly, if an adjustment is not done well, or has no foundation, the effects will add up, year over year, leading to a faulty value conclusion.

Normalization adjustments are changes to the historical financial statements that the valuation analyst makes to reflect the benefits a buyer or investor should expect to receive from the subject company. To expand on this, "[i]f the value of any investment is equal to the present value of its future benefits, determining the appropriate future benefit stream (cash flow) is of primary importance. Therefore, items that are not representative of the appropriate future cash flow must be either eliminated or adjusted in some manner."[71] There are several categories of adjustments, and subtle differences to how they are explained depending on which valuator you are talking to or which valuation text you are reading. I have split normalization adjustments into two general categories that can be observed in most valuations, and specifically, in matrimonial litigation. Those categories are: *control adjustments* (or discretionary adjustments), and *adjustments for non-recurring or accounting convention* related items. Before moving on to explain those two categories, I should note that business valuations can have adjustments for non-operating and/or excess operating assets, and adjustments for tax effects based on the business entity type. These adjustments are sometimes included as normalizing adjustments. Whether or not they are "normalization adjustments" does not matter, but they are, in fact, significant. I will address them in a later chapter.[72]

The first category is control or discretionary adjustments. Interest holders who have a controlling interest have the ability to influence the financial statements of the company in a way that others without control (minority owner) cannot. The focus for this chapter is the income statement. The controlling interest holders can use the company resources, specifically cash, and other obligations in a way that might differ from simple reason, from other businesses in the same industry, or from how a prospective owner might operate the business. These owners have several incentives and reasons for making the decisions in the manner they do. However, in so far as those reasons are not for the benefit of the company, adjustments might be required. A few common examples of control or discretionary normalization adjustments are: reasonable compensation adjustment for officers, rent adjustments for real estate rented from a related party, personal expenses for the benefit of the owners, and expenses for the benefit of related companies. These adjustments are necessary because of the fair market value standard of value, which includes a "willing buyer" concept. A "willing buyer" of the subject company would not "overpay" its expenses. For example, if a company is paying its officers $150,000 when reasonable compensation is $100,000, an adjustment of $50,000 is needed. Additionally, if the company is receiving a benefit that another related company or the owners are paying, that would also require an adjustment. A simple example of this is a business paying below fair market rents to a related party landlord. This rent amount is unreasonable considering that a prospective buyer would be required to pay more in rent. In this case, the normalization adjustment would increase expenses. The last thing to mention before moving to the second category is that the valuation analyst has to decide if control or discretionary adjustments will be made when valuing a non-controlling or minority interest. Returning to the example above of a normalization adjustment for reasonable compensation, if the valuation assignment is for a 25% non-controlling interest, that interest holder would have no ability to reduce the officer's compensation from $150,000 to $100,000. Accordingly, an argument can be made that a normalization adjustment is not warranted in that case. This conversation is related to that of discounts for lack of control, which will be the subject of a subsequent chapter.

The second category of adjustments is for non-recurring items or for accounting conventions. First, let us consider "non-recurring." If the valuator's assignment is to determine the benefits that will be derived in the future, the fact that an income or expense item is "non-recurring" makes it an obvious candidate for adjustment. During the financial statement analysis part of the assignment, any significant fluctuations in income or expenses must be examined to determine the reason for the fluctuation and what the expectation is moving forward. An example of adjustment for a non-recurring item is the forgiveness of Paycheck Protection Program (PPP) loans, which was due to COVID-19. The forgiveness of PPP loans is treated as other income for accounting purposes. The valuation analyst however should exclude this from normalized future income as there is no basis to consider this as recurring income. Also, other income that is not closely tied to the operations of the business (non-operating income) should be removed. While non-operating income may be recurring, it is not connected or derived from operations and, thus, should be removed. It will be considered in the final value conclusion but separate from the capitalization of earnings/cash flows or discounted cash flow part of the income approach.

Second, let us consider "accounting conventions." Adjustments associated with accounting conventions are necessary to reflect an income statement that is free from the effects of the income tax basis of accounting. As discussed in a prior chapter, recording transactions and adjustments according to generally accepted accounting principles (GAAP) and income tax basis are often different. The cash basis of accounting is an option for many small businesses. In these instances, the analyst will have to consider making an adjustment to convert pertinent income and expense accounts from cash to accrual basis. Another common reason for adjustment within this category is accelerated depreciation. The Internal Revenue Code (IRC) allows businesses to accelerate the cost recovery (depreciation) on certain assets. In lieu of recovering the cost through depreciation over the useful lives of the assets, companies can elect to record depreciation for half to all of the cost of the asset in the year the asset is acquired. In these cases, the valuator will adjust the depreciation to reflect commonly used and reasonable depreciable lives. Practically, this means significantly reducing depreciation in the year acquired, and increasing subsequent year's depreciation, to "spread out" the depreciation over the useful life of the asset.

Now that I have introduced the concept and need for normalization adjustments, along with the general categories of adjustments, let's look at the common areas or accounts that commonly require normalization adjustments. Each area or account will include a brief explanation of the need for adjustment, along with an example.[73]

Revenue—These accounts can require adjustments for several reasons. The primary or common reasons include adjusting from cash to accrual basis, and for unusual or non-recurring revenue. In an earlier chapter on the asset approach, I explained that there are two common bases of accounting—GAAP and tax basis. Tax basis will often be treated as synonymous with cash basis. As noted above, the valuation analyst will need to consider adjusting revenue in each historical period to reflect accrual-based GAAP revenue. If the analyst decides to use a capitalization method to arrive at a value of the company through the income approach, this is even more important. Recall that the analyst will likely use multiple historical periods to determine an expected benefit for the future. Further, if a weighted average or trend line-static method is used then having revenue recorded in the period it was actually earned rather than when it was collected is significant. Some valuation analysts may elect to not adjust cash basis revenue. Their rationale is that if revenue and accounts receivable are relatively stable, from year to year, the ultimate effect of the adjustment is, immaterial.

The adjustment from cash basis to accrual basis was illustrated in Figure 7.1. Lastly, I have seen an instance in which the business being valued recorded transactions on the cash basis. The revenue and expenses were relatively flat. The analyst in this case added the accounts receivable at the valuation date to the revenue in the most recent period to "reflect the unrecorded and earned" revenue. Hopefully, her error is apparent. The analyst in this case "doubled up" on the revenue for the most recent period by not subtracting out the accounts receivable at the beginning of the year.

Unusual and or non-recurring revenue is the source of additional adjustments to revenue. While the analyst is trying to determine the benefit stream for the future, she will analyze historical results to assist in determining future benefits. If during this analysis it is revealed that one year has revenue that was unusual in nature and or non-recurring, the analyst will have to consider removing them from her analysis. This is logical as the analyst is trying to determine how the historical performance relates to or is an indicator of future performance. If there was a one-time revenue event, and it is unreasonable to assume that it will recur it should probably be removed. On the other hand, there may be a particular year that saw an unusual *decrease* in revenue due to some unforeseen and likely unrepeated event. In this instance, a business valuator may consider increasing revenue to reflect the revenue absent this event. A good example of an unusual event is COVID. This event had varying effects on companies coupled with governmental assistance programs that had additional significant effects on companies. One example is the restaurant industry. Some of these businesses experienced a significant decline in revenues, but also received assistance from government programs like PPP (Paycheck Protection Program), ERC (Employee Retention Credit), and restaurant grants. In this scenario, a valuation analyst may consider adjusting revenue to what the year was expected to be without COVID-19. Of course, the analyst would have to dig deeper to ascertain if a recovery is possible and how long it will take for that recovery to occur. Additionally, the analyst will need to consider adjusting for the COVID-19 governmental grants. Ultimately, consideration for adjustments to both will be made in tandem.

Cost of Sales or Cost of Goods Sold (COGS)—This group of accounts much like revenue could require adjustments associated with accounting conventions. Many businesses record their transactions and financial statements on the cash basis or some basis other than GAAP. Considerations for these adjustments will likely be connected with adjusting the balance sheet. Two common adjustments in particular are those related to balance sheet considerations for inventory and accounts payable. Remember from our discussion from chapter 7, FIFO (First in, first out) is a better reflection of market value of inventories than LIFO (Last in, first out) is. Accordingly, the analyst may need to adjust COGS in a single or multiple periods to reflect market cost of goods sold. Additionally, as the analysts considers if an adjustment to accounts payable is required, there might need to be a corresponding adjustment to COGS or other expense accounts to better represent COGS as well as selling, general, and administrative costs.

Officer Compensation—Officer compensation, or reasonable compensation, adjustments are among the most common normalization adjustments. This adjustment is also one of the more difficult to make because of its inherent subjectivity. That subjectivity can land this adjustment in the crosshairs of an opposing valuator or litigator. Complicating the matter even more in matrimonial litigation contexts is the concept of "double dipping." The "double dipping" concept results from cases where there are both equitable distribution and spousal support components applicable. Spousal support is directly affected by the compensation of the spouse working in the business. Additionally, the business valuation is directly affected by the determination of reasonable compensation. Therefore, the spousal support calculations should be adjusted in connection with the officer compensation adjustment made in the business valuation. Consider this brief example to illustrate the concept. Assume that a business was paying the officer/owner $150,000. During the course of the business valuation, the valuation analyst determined that reasonable compensation was $100,000. This change would reduce expenses, increase income, and ultimately increase the value of the company and potential marital property. Accordingly, if the spousal support calculations do not adjust in some way for this change, "double dipping" will have occurred where one spouse receives *both* one half of a higher value of the business *and* spousal support based on a higher *unreasonable* salary.

The goal for the valuator (as with all adjustments) is to remove as much of the subjectivity as possible, resulting in a reasonable compensation figure. This, however, is not an exact science. There are myriad factors affecting the determination of reasonable compensation. A brief non-exhaustive list of factors to consider are: industry of the business, geographic location whether rural or urban, years of experience, existence of managers/supervisors, duties and hours worked, proficiency of the individual, profitability of the company, and size of the company.

So, what will a valuator do in adjusting officer compensation to reflect a reasonable amount? Typically, the valuator will consider the information gathered in the management interview, company and industry analysis, and from compensation data. Information gathered from these sources can be used to determine the reasonable compensation amount. The management interview is an important part of this process. Among other things, it will help determine the role and duties of the officers, their experience, how much assistance—or lack thereof—they get from other members of management or leadership, hours worked, and their estimate of reasonable or replacement compensation. The analyst also needs to reflect upon her financial analysis of the company, and how the company relates to the industry. Is the company more profitable than the industry norm? Why is that? Is it because of the one officer, or the team around them, or perhaps a significantly profitable product line? The answers to those questions, and many more, should influence the ultimate decision on reasonable compensation. Finally, the analyst should consider market compensation data. There are several potential sources for this data, for example: RMA Data (Risk Management Association), RCReports (Reasonable Compensation Reports), MGMA (Physician compensation data), as well as other publications and surveys readily available (for example the American Dental Association data). The valuation analyst will use her professional judgement in considering the fact pattern and all of the information available to her in determining an appropriate amount for reasonable compensation. Lastly, it should be noted that the compensation determined to be reasonable includes fringe benefits and retirement benefits. These expenses, when applicable, may be recorded in other accounts. The valuation analyst will need to remove these expenses through normalization adjustments. Finally, the normalization adjustment for reasonable compensation will have a related effect on payroll taxes that should also be considered.

Rent Expense—If the business being valued is renting its real estate from a related party, the valuation analyst must consider if the rent being paid is fair market rent. Much like compensation, an officer/ owner can have several reasons for paying rent either in excess or below fair market rents. When either of these occurs, the valuation analyst should consider making an adjustment. What is fair market rent? This question, like officers compensation, will force the analyst to seek help. The best help is a real estate appraisal that provides the fair value of the real estate as well as fair market rents. In cases where an appraisal is available, the adjustment for fair market rents will lean heavily on the appraisal. Appraisals are not always available due to cost restraints. In cases such as this the analyst will consider other sources of information.

Those sources include the historical cost, the county tax assessed value, and any available information from commercial real estate agents. Judgement must be exercised on behalf of the valuation analyst in determining the appropriate fair market rent from the information available. When an appraisal is not available and the valuation analyst has to depend on additional, less authoritative sources, she will likely cite this reality in the assumptions and limiting conditions portion of the report. After all, the decision to obtain a real estate appraisal is not a decision to be made by the analyst. While not a limiting condition in the theoretical sense of the word, the conclusion of value of a business could be different if an appraisal were attained.

Depreciation—The purpose of depreciation is to reflect cost recovery of fixed assets, or those assets that are capitalized and recorded on the balance sheet. Traditionally, there are two primary methods of recording depreciation, book basis and tax basis. Book basis depreciation intends to what we said, reflect the recovery of the cost of the asset over a reasonable period. Tax basis depreciation can be significantly different, often accelerating the cost recovery. There are certain provisions in the Internal Revenue Code (IRC) that allow businesses to recover all or a significant portion of the cost in the first year. In these instances, the valuation analyst may choose to decrease the first-year depreciation and spread accelerated portion over the remaining useful life of the asset. This is especially important when the analyst uses the weighted average or trend line-static method to estimate the benefits into the future. If the depreciation is not adjusted, or spread out, it could distort the benefit available to an investor.

Amortization—The purpose of amortization is to reflect the reasonable cost recovery of intangible assets. The common intangible assets that are amortized on are leasehold improvements and goodwill. Leasehold improvements occur when a tenant incurs significant expenses to make improvements to the space that they are renting. Those costs are recovered in the form of amortization, usually over fifteen years. Some business valuators may consider removing the amortization. Important factors in that determination include: what is the remaining lease term, is the lessor a related party, and what was the source of the fair rent adjustment if leasing from a related party. In addition to leasehold improvements, some businesses have goodwill on their balance sheet resulting from prior purchases of businesses or books of business. These costs are recovered in the form of amortization, usually over fifteen years. The amortization related to goodwill should be removed. The rationale for this is based upon the intention to value the current business at the current valuation date, including the goodwill from the current business at the current valuation date. If amortization from previously acquired businesses is included in the normalized earnings or cash flows it could have an unintended effect on the valuation.

Personal Expenses—Another common source of normalization adjustments are personal expenses, or those for the benefit of officers and owners. These expenses are discretionary and have no business purpose, and accordingly should be removed. In effect, they are additional compensation. Personal expenses come in many forms but most often appear or are reflected in the following expense accounts: compensation to a non-working spouse, compensation to children who are not working in the business, telephone, travel, entertainment, auto, and legal and professional fees.

Miscellaneous Income—Miscellaneous income by name or nature is of the sort that the valuation analyst should review to determine if it should be removed. If the income is routine and/or connected with central revenue drivers of a business, it would likely be included as revenue and not adjustments. However, if the miscellaneous income is unusual, recognized infrequently, and or clearly associated with a non-operating asset, the valuation analyst should consider if a normalizing adjustment is warranted.

Normalization adjustments, their foundation, execution, and defense can have a significant effect on any valuation and litigation event. Valuation analysts, have a significant responsibility. They must convince the users of business valuation reports that the adjustments were both warranted in fact and reasonable in amount. They should explain their adjustments thoroughly in the report so that the user of the report would come to the same conclusion.

The previous chapter introduced the income approach. This chapter established the foundation for normalization adjustments, categories of adjustments, and a brief list of accounts and areas that commonly require normalization adjustments. The next chapter will complete our discussion on the income approach, focusing on the denominator of the present value formula, rate of return, or as I will refer to it: discount rate and capitalization rate.

CHAPTER 10

DISCOUNT RATE AND CAPITALIZATION RATE

For the past two chapters I have been discussing the income approach. First in chapter eight I introduced the approach. That introduction included explaining the theory behind the income approach at a high level—which is to view the subject company as an investment. What amount of returns or benefits in the future would be required for someone to invest in the company with the understanding that every proposed return or benefit has an associated level of risk? This question, theory, and ultimate value through the income approach is summed up well through a formula.

$$\text{Value} = \frac{\text{Benefits}}{\text{Rate of Return}}$$

In chapter eight, I also discussed several commonly used methods used within the income approach to produce a value to be considered in a value conclusion. The previous chapter explained normalization adjustments, which directly affect the numerator in the formula above. In the present chapter, I will focus on the denominator, what I have labeled above as "rate of return." Expanding from there, it is understood as the required rate of return or cost of capital that is related to the benefits reflected in the numerator. Every investment has a benefit and related risk, and the two are related. The rate of return or cost of capital is typically expressed as a discount rate or capitalization rate depending on the method used to determine value within the income approach. This chapter will introduce those two rates, thus, bringing our discussion of the income approach to a close.

There are probably many apt metaphors to explain cost of capital or rate of return. As we will see below, there are a lot of elements of cost of capital and rate of return. However, one lighthearted metaphor comes to mind—"I double dog dare you." This ultimate challenge has been referenced in movies, is believed to have been around for more than a century, and has likely been used by you or a friend. Strangely enough, this dare can be helpful in explaining cost of capital. The person being dared in these situations was faced with a very difficult task, probably without any benefit or reward. However, there are in fact rewards or benefits to be received after the dare was completed. For one, the person being dared will have "risen to the occasion" (as a parent writing this, I cringe) and that in and of itself has certain benefits. Furthermore, the person being dared is thinking to himself, if I do this, there will be benefits of some sort in the future. In that moment the person being dared evaluates the risk of the dare against the future benefits resulting from the decision to engage in the dare (to invest or not). Hence, the rate of return.[74]

The subject of this chapter, if handled in detail, could make it one of the longest chapters in the book. My handling of it will be a bit different, a more abridged version. In my condensed address, I will discuss the following: define and describe cost of capital, describe elements of discount rates, and introduce methods to determine the cost of capital. I believe this outline will provide you with what you need in understanding the denominator of the equation above, the risk or rate of return required for investment in a company.

What is cost of capital and rate of return? To help answer that question and aid in our discussion, I have included comments on this subject from two well-known business valuators. Their comments will serve as the talking points to explain cost of capital and rate of return.

- "The cost of capital is also referred to as the discount rate. It equals the total expected rate of return for the investment, that is, dividends or withdrawals, plus expected capital appreciation over the life of the investments. This rate, when applied to the appropriate income or cash flow stream of a company, will give an estimate of the company's value."[75]
- "The amount of risk that is perceived by the market must generally be balanced by the rate of return that is offered for the investment in order to entice investors to take the risk of making the investment. Stated differently, if a willing buyer wants to make an investment in a closely held company, the rate of return being offered, based on the price to be paid for the investment, must be high enough to justify taking the risk."[76]

One of the first things you will note is that cost of capital is linked to the discount rate, not the capitalization rate. This can be confusing as some times these terms are used interchangeably. But they are indeed different. The discount rate is equal to the capitalization rate *plus* the long-term growth rate. This makes sense if we remember that present value is equal to benefits divided by rate of return. The benefits in that formula are in the future, accordingly, the logical factor to use is the discount rate. The application of the discount rate will return future benefits to the present value. This does not mean that the capitalization rate should not be used. It simply means that there is a starting point, and, as we have discussed above, there are two methods to choose: discounting methods and capitalization methods.

The next thing you might notice is the comprehensive nature of the return that the discount rate is accounting for. It is the total return, including distributions and dividends, but also the capital appreciation that is not distributed each year. Instead that amount is retained to be used in the future growth of the company. Also included in that same sentence above, the return contemplates the returns "over the life of the investments."[77]

The cost of capital must consider both the inherent risk associated with any stream of benefits and the investors' expectations of returns on an investment. As you know, risk and return have a symbiotic relationship. As risk increases, investors require a greater possible return. Conversely, as risk decreases, investors require less return. Therefore, the benefits and return (the basic elements introduced in the formula above) must be related. The return, or cost of capital, cannot be a generic factor. No, it must be specific to the estimated benefits. Only then would a willing buyer and willing seller agree upon a price.

I have mentioned risk several times, but what are these risks? Good question! I have included a list below including ten risk factors. The list is not exhaustive but helps to illustrate the considerations before the analyst.[78]

- Economic risk
- Business risk
- Operating risk
- Financial risk
- Asset risk
- Product risk
- Market risk
- Technological risk

- Regulatory risk
- Legal risk

I will now introduce the individual elements used to calculate the discount and capitalization rates. They are as follows: risk-free rate, equity risk premium, size premium, industry risk premium, company specific premium, beta, and finally, growth rate.

- **Risk-free Rate**—The risk-free rate, also known as the safe rate, is the "rate of return available in the market on an investment free of default risk."[79] A starting point for many analysts in determining the discount rate is the risk-free rate. It is a baseline indicator of return on the safest of investments. There are several sources of this rate such as estimated long-term Treasury Bill rates. The selection of this rate should be selected in tandem with the methodology used to select the equity risk premium.

- **Equity Risk Premium**—The equity risk premium is "a rate of return added to a risk-free rate to reflect the additional risk of equity instruments over risk-free instruments (a component of the cost of equity capital or equity discount rate)."[80] If an investor chooses to invest in Apple or General Motors for instance, that investment carries additional risk over and above that of a "risk-free" investment such as a Treasury Bill. Accordingly, it requires a greater return as well, and that is the equity risk premium.

- **Size Premium**—The equity risk premium and estimated total equity return is that of large companies such as Apple or General Motors in keeping with the example above. In general, there is more risk in smaller companies than fortune 500 companies. Not many people would argue against that. There are many factors that lead to that conclusion, but on the whole, it is widely accepted as true as evidenced by the investments of the general public. That additional risk is accompanied by additional returns, and referred to as the size premium in consideration of the discount rate.

- **Industry Risk Premium**—Some industries are inherently more or less risky than the majority of industries. Much like the equity risk premium and size premium, where there is greater risk it is reflected in greater returns. Those expected greater returns are reflected in the industry risk premium.

- **Company Specific Premium**—Thus far in discussing the different indicators of additional risk and required returns, we have covered the gamut: types of investments, fixed income or equities, small companies versus larger companies, industries that carry additional risk or conversely are less risky than the general investment spectrum. Each of these premiums or factors addresses elements of risk within a subject company. But is that all the potential risk of a company? If you said, "probably not," you would be correct. The company specific premium is intended to reflect the additional risk for the particular subject company being valued. I have included a non-exhaustive list from Shannon Pratt and Alina Niculita of potential risk factors influencing the analyst's conclusions on the company specific premium.[81]
  - o Management depth
  - o Management expertise
  - o Access to capital
  - o Customer concentration
  - o Customer pricing leverage
  - o Customer loyalty and stability
  - o Level of current competition
  - o Potential new competitors
  - o Supplier concentration
  - o Supplier pricing advantage

- o Product or service diversification
- o Life cycle of current products or services
- o Geographical distribution
- o Demographics
- o Availability of labor
- o Employee stability
- o Internal and external culture
- o Economic factors
- o Industry and government regulations
- o Political factors
- o Fixed assets' age and condition
- o Strength of intangible assets
- o Distribution system
- o IT systems
- o Technological life cycle
- o Location
- o Legal/litigation issues
- o Internal controls
- o Currency risk

- **Beta**—This is "a measure of systematic risk of a stock; the tendency of a stock's price to correlate with changes in a specific index."[82] Beta can be used to adjust the equity risk premium to give effect for how the subject company may be different than a particular index that the equity risk premium is derived from.
- **Growth rate**—The growth rate represents the expected long-term growth of the company. It is important to emphasize the phrase "long-term" in that sentence. The selected growth rate that will be subtracted from the discount rate to result in the capitalization rate is the expected returns into perpetuity. The growth rate is the difference in the discount and capitalization

rates. Another important aspect in the selection of an appropriate growth rate is the consideration of nominal versus real growth. Nominal growth includes considerations for inflation growth and non-inflation growth which is understood as "real" growth. Selecting a growth rate equal to the inflation rate essentially indicates that there will not be any real growth. Additionally, selecting a growth rate above the historic growth of the GDP of the United States may be difficult to defend. This would in essence be saying that the subject company is going to outpace the entire spectrum of investments into perpetuity.[83]

So how does the analyst use these elements to estimate the cost of capital? There are several methods but two that are most commonly used and covered briefly below.

- **Build-up Method**—The build-up method (BUM) is commonly used in small and medium sized companies. This method determines the discount rate by adding or "building" up the different elements of risk noted above. This is illustrated in the table below.

Risk-free rate	3.50%
Equity risk premium	5.50%
Size premium	5.75%
Industry risk premium	0.25%
Company specific risk premium	4.00%
Discount rate	19.00%

An advantage to this method is its relative simplicity in concept and the availability of data for all but one of the elements.

- **Weighted Average Cost of Capital**—The weighted average cost of capital (WACC) method produces a cost of capital that is determined through considering the cost of debt and cost of equity individually and separately. Then taking an appropriate weighted average of the two. The formula for this method is illustrated in the table below.

WACC	=	(Cost of Equity X Weight of Equity)	+	(Cost of Debt X Weight of Debt)

An advantage of this method is that it bifurcates the company's capital and assigns a specific cost to both individual components. One difficult element, or often discussed dilemma, with this method is what weights to use between the two sources of capital. There are two possible options. First, the analyst can base his decision on weightings based on the historical balance sheets of the company. This can be problematic if there is no consistent mix of capital between equity and debt. The other possibility is to use a hypothetical debt to equity structure. This is reasonable when we remember the "willing buyer" concept introduced as part of the definition of fair market value. In this case, the valuation analyst will use a capital structure that will produce the results and lowest costs because this is what a "reasonable buyer" would do.

Hopefully, by this point some things are clear as it relates to the discount rate and capitalization rates. First, discount and capitalization rates are not the same. Discount rates are the starting point. The capitalization rate is a derivation of the discount rate resulting from subtracting the long-term growth rate from the discount rate.[84] There are several tools used to develop the discount rate but the two you will likely see used the most are the BUM and WACC. Each of these are reasonable methods to be used and have instances where one or the other may be more appropriate.

The importance of determining an appropriate cost of capital cannot be overstated. What appears to be small or subtle changes can change the value by thousands or millions of dollars. As a user of the valuation report, you need to be able to understand the method that the analyst used to determine the discount rate. Being able to understand and evaluate the analyst's selection of a company specific premium will also be important to you. My hope is that this chapter helped in that regard.

This chapter was the final in a series of three introducing the income approach. This approach is frequently used and understandably so. Seldom will you see a valuation report where, in arriving at the final value, the analyst did not weight the income approach at all. In addition to the income and asset approaches, there is one additional approach, the market approach. This approach is a completely different way of determining a value of a company, leaning heavily on external data to support the conclusion of value for a company. This is reasonable and logical, especially when we remember the "willing buyer" and "willing seller" components of the definition of fair market value.

CHAPTER 11

MARKET APPROACH

In this chapter, I will introduce the market approach—the third and final approach used in business valuations. Its inclusion as the third or last should not be interpreted as a reflection on its validity. It is significant to the appraisal engagement and should receive appropriate attention and weight in the eyes of the user. The inclusion of the phrase "willing buyer" and "willing seller" in the definition of fair market value contributes to the argument for the applicability of the market approach. After all, an approach that is premised with applying data to the subject company is to be considered. This chapter will introduce the process that is the market approach. This includes selecting subject company data to be used, identifying relevant market data to be applied, and, finally, applying any necessary adjustments to result in a value of the company through the market approach.

My oldest son is fifteen and is eager to get behind the wheel and have his own vehicle. He asked if he could have my truck when he turns sixteen. I told him that he could buy it from me and that we would "work out a deal." The first thing he had to do was figure out how much it was worth. I showed him a few websites that would provide the value of the truck. Those websites have a lot of questions that help to determine the value of that particular truck. The market approach is similar to this. There are various sources of information available to the appraiser to assist in determining the value of a company. Like my son, the appraiser has to know the subject company being appraised, how it is similar and dissimilar to other businesses to determine the appropriate value.

The market approach can be defined as "a general way of determining a value indication of a business, business ownership, security, or intangible asset by using one or more methods that compare the subject to similar businesses, business ownership interests, securities, or intangible assets that have been sold."[85] In theory this is pretty straight forward. The appraiser is tasked with identifying the data from "similar businesses," which we will refer to as a market multiple or multiplier, and then applying it to the subject company. Another benefit, besides simplicity and the understandable nature of this approach, is that the market multiples are based on actual sales transactions and public company data. This contributes to the validity of this approach and value just as when market sales data is used in real estate appraisals. As attractive as the approach can be, there are also times when an analyst would object to or caution its use. There are situations in which the number of transactions for similar companies is limited. This is cause for concern. Another common concern is the data itself. Much of the data included in the databases that analysts use comes from business brokers. The expertise of the broker and analyst is not the same, and so how data is defined and understood is not always similar. Further, there is a limited amount of data provided on the similar businesses that have sold. These limitations might lead the analyst to use the market approach only as a "sanity check," corroborating method, or apply less weight to the market approach than that of another approach.

How do you apply the market method? The analyst first must understand the subject company. This is no different than the application of the other two approaches but necessary to state up front. The analyst who spends little time on the market approach and slaps a market multiplier on some data from the subject company is prone to error. The analyst first needs to have a firm grip on understanding the subject company. This includes its industry and if there are significant multiple product lines within the company. It is helpful as well to identify if the business is operating in a rural or urban context, its geographical home (i.e., southeast, mid-west, etc.), if it has a single location or multiple locations, and more. Fortunately, the analyst should know all of this information as it was gathered early on in the process.

There are several methods of determining the value of a company through the market approach. I have listed them below and included a brief discussion of each.

- **Guideline Company Transaction Method**—This method is also referred to as the merger and acquisition method. It is a method "whereby pricing multiples are derived from transactions of significant interest in companies engaged in the same or similar lines of business."[86] I listed this method first because it is used most frequently of those listed. That is because the number of small and mid-sized companies being valued outweighs larger companies, and most of the transaction data available is for smaller private companies that have sold. There are several databases that acquire and compile data that can be used to create multiples and multipliers to apply to the subject company. The following are some of the more frequently used databases:
  - BIZCOMPS
  - ValuSource Market Comps
  - Mergerstat

    o   DoneDeals Comps

    o   DealStats™

- **Guideline Public Company Method**—This is the method "whereby market multiples are derived from market prices of companies that are engaged in the same or similar lines of business, and that are actively traded on a free and open market."[87] The Guideline Company Transaction Method uses data from publicly traded companies to determine multiples and multipliers. The financial data on public companies is readily available to the public due to the financial reporting requirements of the SEC. There are services available that help with producing industry lists and pulling together the data for the analyst.

- There are two other methods that you might see included in business valuation reports—internal transaction and industry rule of thumb. These methods are not used as often as the first two listed.

    o   **Internal Transaction**—This method is as it states—data from prior sales of the subject company stock is used to determine the value at a subsequent point. A key consideration here is whether the transaction was an arm's length transaction. Was the transaction conducted in a manner similar to the way unrelated parties would design a transaction. If not, it should be reviewed closely to determine if it can be used. There are other considerations: what is similar or dissimilar from prior transactions about the company, about the economy, about the industry, and more?

    o   **Industry Rule of Thumb**—There are some industries that have established rules of thumb. One example is the dental industry. The rule of thumb is that the value of a dental practice is generally equal to 60%-70% of revenue. Of course, there are outliers, but most will end up in that range. Business valuators will seldom rely solely on industry rule of thumbs. However, they are a good and helpful sanity check to the values established by the income and market approaches. In the event that there are differences, the analyst needs to investigate, understand, and be able to articulate why.

I have introduced the methods within the approach and discussed where the data comes from for application in the market approach. Now, I will discuss what data is available through these databases and how appraisers select the appropriate data for the valuation of the subject company. Depending on the NAICS (North American Industry Classification System) or SIC (Standard Industrial Classification) code, there will be varying numbers of transactions. On any given transaction, the following will be reported: annual revenue, SDE (Sellers' discretionary earnings), inventory, FF&E (Furniture, fixtures & equipment), number of employees, asking price, selling price, sale terms, sale date, location, age of business, income statement and balance sheet, type of sale (asset or stock), and more.

To illustrate the type of information available through these databases I have included excerpts below. They reflect transaction data from the SIC code 1541—General Contractors—Industrial Buildings and Warehouses. The two excerpts are from BIZCOMPS and DealStats™, respectively.[88]

Figure 11.1 - Excerpt of Data Available from the BIZCOMP database									
Admin	Subject Business								
ID	SIC	NAICS	Business Description	Revenue	SDE	Inventory	FF&E	Rent/ Revenue	Employees
00623	1541	236220	Contr-Bldg Ren.	1,465	366	80	50	4.4%	6
00624	1541	236220	Contr-Comm.	1,321	284	0	150	1.0%	31
00619	1541	236220	Contr-Comm.	844	284	1	215		6
00620	1541	236220	Contr-Comm.	760	229	0	1	0.4%	4
00621	1541	236220	Contr-Comm.	480	132	2	105		4
00622	1541	236220	Contr-Comm.	592	53	30	30		4
00618	1541	238220	Contr-Gen Comm.	3,200	1,500	600	750		28

Admin	Transaction							
ID	Asking Price	Price	Price / Revenue	Price / SDE	Down Pmt	Terms	Days on Mkt	Sale Date
00623	569	330	0.23	0.90	50%			1/30/2012
00624	495	475	0.36	1.67				1/20/2012
00619	750	725	0.86	2.55	100%			2/22/2020
00620	125	120	0.16	0.52	17%	10 Yrs @ 6%		7/5/2014
00621	325	270	0.56	2.05	100%			4/29/2014
00622	99	74	0.13	1.40	59%	5 Yrs @ 65		11/5/2013
00618	6,400	1,900	0.59	1.27	100%			2/26/2020

Admin	Location				
ID	Location	State	Census Region	Census Division	Other Area
00623	Florida	FL	South	South Atlantic	East
00624	Florida	FL	South	South Atlantic	East
00619	Oregon	OR	West	Pacific	Northwest
00620	Florida	FL	South	South Atlantic	East
00621	Florida	FL	South	South Atlantic	East
00622	Florida	FL	South	South Atlantic	East
00618	NV	NV	West	Mountain	Southwest

Figure 11.2 - Excerpt of Data Available from the DealStats™ database							
Statistic	Count	Range	10th Percentile	25th Percentile	Median	75th Percentile	90th Percentile
Sale Date	10	02/05/2001 — 05/07/2021					
Net Sales	10	$591,686 — $10,039,000	$716,613	$1,211,474	$1,930,915	$3,663,891	$5,633,973
MVIC Price	10	$74,200 — $3,000,000	$97,420	$418,750	$590,960	$1,642,500	$2,572,500
EBITDA	6	$8,537 — $694,924	$13,856	$31,062	$144,638	$529,638	$663,462
Seller's Discretionary Earnings (SDE)	10	($33,607) — $846,924	$43,688	$79,003	$268,936	$600,024	$816,392
Gross Profit Margin	6	10.5% — 84.4%	12.30%	15.00%	26.20%	42.40%	64.70%
SDE Margin	10	(2.0%) — 38.3%	3.80%	7.50%	10.30%	17.00%	22.30%
EBITDA Margin	6	0.7% — 16.9%	1.90%	3.10%	4.80%	11.70%	15.20%
Operating Profit Margin	10	0.2% — 14.8%	2.80%	3.30%	4.60%	8.70%	13.40%
Net Profit Margin	8	2.6% — 13.3%	3.10%	4.00%	5.30%	10.50%	13.20%
MVIC/Net Sales	10	0.09x — 0.92x	0.13	0.21	0.32	0.44	0.61
MVIC/Gross Profit	6	0.28x — 2.40x	0.36	0.47	0.84	1.52	2.04
MVIC/EBIT	10	2.4x — 52.2x	3.7	4.2	5.5	8.8	22.1
MVIC/EBITDA	6	2.1x — 11.7x	3	3.9	4.2	5.6	8.9
MVIC/SDE	9	1.4x — 3.5x	1.7	1.9	2.6	2.8	3.2
MVIC/Book Value of Invested Capital	1	2.5x — 2.5x	2.5	2.5	2.5	2.5	2.5

The analyst has to exercise judgement in deciding which companies from the initial population will be selected to be used to determine the market multiples and multipliers. The initial search results will typically include a lot of different companies. The factors to consider include, but are not limited to: location or geography, size, profitability, date of sale, and revenue. Typically, analysts will start with some general parameters for paring down the data. For example, the analyst may choose data for the past five years, or ten years. Or may include companies that have from fifty percent of revenue to five times the revenue of the subject company. Sometimes the analyst might be forced to broaden her criteria or range to produce additional transactions to have a sufficient number to make a valid population. No one company is exactly the same as the subject company, so it is better to have more transactions. The analyst also needs to consider the variability of the data. Statistical measures of standard deviation and coefficient of variation are important here. These statistical measures indicate the degree of dispersion of the data in a population. A lower dispersion of data generally reflects a better population of market multiples, and increases confidence in the resulting value produced by the market approach. As you can see, the analyst has to exercise professional judgement in determining which transactions make it into the population of selected data. Ultimately, the selected transactions from one analyst to another may differ, but all decisions must be supported by reason and should result in similar values produced by the market approach.

Once the analyst has determined what transactions will be selected, she must decide which multiple(s) to use. Depending on the source of transactions, there could be any or all of the following multipliers or multiples resulting from the selected transactions:

- **Price to Revenue**—This multiple is determined by dividing the purchase price by the company revenue.

- **Price to Gross Profit**—Determined by subtracting cost of goods sold, or those direct costs of production (i.e., direct labor, materials, and miscellaneous expenses) from revenue.
- **Price to EBIT**—EBIT stands for earnings before interest and taxes.
- **Price to EBITDA**—EBITDA stands for earnings before interest, taxes, depreciation, and amortization.
- **Price to Discretionary Earnings**—Discretionary earnings (SDE or DE) or cash flows as it can be referred to, is generally understood as being EBITDA plus officers' compensation.

Each of these multiples and multipliers can be appropriate and reasonable to use, and must be evaluated by the analyst on a case-by-case basis. EBIT, EBITDA, and SDE tend to be used more frequently because they are indicators of profitability, earnings, or efficiency of a business. Gross profit can do this as well, though to a lesser degree. Revenue has its place as well, but the resulting value will not be based on any measure of profitability. In summary, the analyst must exercise their judgement in applying the appropriate multiples.

The last part of our discussion about selecting market multiples deals with which mathematical multiple the analyst will use. Will she use a simple average of the Price to Revenue multiple or the median? Analysts typically elect to use the median as opposed to the mean, or average. The reason is that the median is less influenced by outliers and is generally thought to be a better indicator of central tendency. But that is not the end of the conversation. Often, the valuation analyst will need to consider using a multiple less than or greater than the median (for example, the 10th percentile, 25th percentile, 75th percentile, or 90th percentile). This decision should be supported by an analysis of company and industry data. It is possible that the subject company is significantly more profitable than the industry. If that is the case, the analyst may consider using the 75th or 90th percentile data, or some multiple greater than the median, and vice versa. Again, judgement and expertise are required by the business valuator. The multiple used should be consistent with other aspects of the valuation and reflective of a company that is performing better or worse than the norm.

After deciding which multiple(s) to use, the analyst will have to determine what subject company data the multiple will be applied to, and what adjustments are necessary to this data. The analyst has to decide what year or years, and weighting, of subject company data will be used to apply the market multiples to. I discussed this concept in an earlier chapter on the income approach. The theory here is similar and we will cover it here briefly. As an example, let us assume that the analyst wants to apply the price to revenue multiple. What revenue is the analyst going to apply the market multiple to? The most recent year from the subject company? Or perhaps the last three years? Additionally, the analyst has to decide how to weight these years. Will she use a simple average, or, instead, elect to weight them unevenly to reflect a perceived trend in the historical data?

Finally, after the analyst has applied the selected market multiple to the subject company data she must then consider if any adjustments are necessary. Depending on the database used, the market multiples produced might be reflective of transactions that include or exclude the transfer of working capital for instance. Working capital is the current assets of a company less current liabilities. Accordingly, if market data does not include the transfer of working capital, the analyst would have to add back working capital of the subject company to produce an accurate result from the market approach. I have included an example on the next page to illustrate the application of the market approach.

Figure 11.3 - Example of the Application of the Market Approach	
Revenue - Year Ended December 31, 2020	1,250,000
Revenue - Year Ended December 31, 2019	1,325,000
Revenue - Year Ended December 31, 2018	1,195,000
Selected Company Revenue	1,256,667
Price to Revenue Multiple	0.47
Subtotal	590,633
Adjustments:	
Cash	125,000
Accounts receivable	147,500
Accounts payable	(89,000)
Other current liabilities	(50,000)
Total adjustments	133,500
Selected Value, rounded	724,100

As with many areas of the business valuation assignment, judgement and expertise of the analyst must be used. There are many opportunities within the market approach for errors to be made. Done well, the market approach adds a significant element to the valuation, and increases confidence in the conclusion of value to the user of the business valuation. The valuation report should include a narrative and information as to how the market approach was applied such that the user of the report understands the foundation behind the application of the approach. Be sure as a user of the report to review closely and follow the methodology and logic of the report so that you can have confidence in the results of the market approach and value conclusion of the subject company.

This chapter concludes a series of five chapters where I introduced the three approaches used in business valuations. In the next chapter, I will introduce discounts for lack of control and lack of marketability. Like the market approach, there are many difficulties within the process of determining if a discount applies, and if so, what the discount should be. Fortunately, the introduction and discussion in this text will be abbreviated and lighter than the treatises that exist.

CHAPTER 12

DISCOUNTS FOR LACK OF CONTROL AND LACK OF MARKETABILITY

This chapter could be considered one of the most technical in the book. Some, a lot, or even most of the subjects and aspects of previous chapters are seemingly settled and generally agreed to in the valuation community. That is not the case with discounts. That underscores the difficulty ahead of us. The subjects of discounts for lack of control (DLOC) and lack of marketability (DLOM) are the primary matters at hand in this chapter. I will also touch on premiums, though they are seldom seen in valuations of small and mid-sized companies in North Carolina family law cases.

A simple example should illustrate the significance of this discussion and the conclusions or opinions of analysts. In the example on the next page, I have assumed that both experts arrived at the same income approach value. Expert #1 used combined discounts of 25% (though not additive, we will discuss this later in the chapter). Expert

#2 used combined discounts of 55%. This results in a difference in the two conclusions of $600,000 or 31%.

Figure 12.1 - Illustrative Example of Differing Conclusions Based on Application of Discounts		
	Expert #1	Expert #2
Value from Income Approach	2,500,000	2,500,000
Discount for Lack of Control	10%	30%
Marketable, minority value	2,250,000	1,750,000
Discount for Lack of Marketability	15%	25%
Minority, non-marketable value	1,912,500	1,312,500
Difference in Value		600,000
% Difference in Value		31%

At my first job in public accounting I heard this saying, "You don't learn anything on the easy ones." Although not a great use of the English language, it has stuck with me. The partner who said it was trying to encourage me to push deeper and further in my technical knowledge. In addition, he was trying to instill within me a habit of embracing challenges because that is where growth occurs. In my present firm, I find myself encouraging others much in the same way. It would be easy and expedient for a valuation analyst to "slap" a 20% DLOC and a 25% DLOM on a value, add some boilerplate language to a report, and move on. This is dangerous. The analyst should dig in, understand the elements that are driving the potential discounts and assign an appropriate and defensible discount. For you, a matrimonial attorney, understanding the theory, common application, and sources of support for discounts is important in your role and helpful through the equitable distribution process.

In this chapter we will focus on the theory behind the discounts, target a basic level of understanding, delve deeper where needed for matrimonial litigation in North Carolina, and provide a brief explanation of the sources and tools available to analysts to determine a DLOC and DLOM. The starting point for our discussion will be to introduce the spectrum of levels of value. This is a phrase that represents the different types of interests to be valued in any engagement.

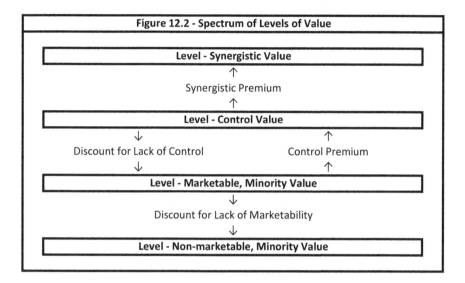

Figure 12.2 - Spectrum of Levels of Value

In this version of the spectrum, you can see four levels of value along with the discount or premium representing the difference in each level.[89] For purposes of explaining the spectrum, let us call the control value the base level. This is the value of a company without consideration for lack of control, lack of marketability, and additional value (a premium) associated with synergies. In order for the control value to be the base level we need to also assume that the asset, income, and market approaches produce a control value. This is one of many areas that can be a source for disagreement within the discounts and premiums discussion. For this assumption to be true, I want to provide a brief comment on this subject for each of the three approaches.[90]

- **Asset Approach**—There is not much discussion regarding the asset approach—the consensus is that it produces a control value.

- **Income Approach**—The income approach can produce a control value or a minority value. As I noted in chapter nine on normalization adjustments, a key factor is control adjustments. If the analyst makes adjustments to the historical financial statements irrespective of the fact that the interest being valued might or might not have control, the ultimate value produced will be a control value. If, however, the adjustments were not made (where a minority interest is being valued) because the holder would not have the ability to implement them, the resulting value would be a minority value.

- **Market Approach**—The market approach could produce a control value, synergistic value, or a marketable, minority value. If the analyst uses guideline public company data, the traditional understanding of the resulting value is marketable minority value. However, that subject is debated among some valuators. On the other hand, if the analyst is using guideline company data or the merger and acquisition method, the resulting value will most likely be control value. One caveat: the resulting value could also be a synergistic value, but rarely is.

To the base level, control value, some buyers are willing to pay *more* for a business than FMV. This is an example of a premium. A buyer is incentivized to do this when there is a synergistic or strategic reason for doing so. There might be infrastructure in place in the acquiring company such that upon acquisition the acquired company can immediately be more profitable once brought "into the fold" of the acquiring company. Synergistic value can also be called strategic value, or investment value. That last phrase, investment value, is important. As we discussed in a previous chapter, this is a premise of value to the holder, separate from value in exchange or fair market value. For North Carolina matrimonial litigation, there are not many scenarios where synergistic value and its related premium would need to be applied.

In between the control value, and marketable, minority value is the term "control premium." In instances where the resulting value from the income or market approaches resulted in a marketable, minority value, the analyst would need to add to that value a premium reflective of the additional value associated with control.

Lastly, I would like to reiterate that there is a significant amount of discussion on these matters. That is important because even the spectrum of levels of value presented above could be presented differently by different analysts. For example, some analysts would argue that in specific instances a discount for lack of marketability should apply to control values for smaller companies. That level of value is not reflected in the spectrum above. Proponents of a discount for controlling interests would note that "controlling interests are far less liquid than an actively traded security, although in most cases they are more liquid than a private minority position."[91]

DISCOUNTS FOR LACK OF CONTROL

As we move into our introduction of discounts for lack of control, I have included the common terms and definitions pertinent to the discussion. These definitions come from the International Glossary of Business Valuation Terms.[92]

- **Control**—The power to direct the management and policies of a business enterprise.
- **Control Premium**—An amount or a percentage by which the pro rata value of a controlling interest exceeds the pro rata value of a non-controlling interest in a business enterprise, to reflect the power of control.
- **Discount for Lack of Control**—An amount or percentage deducted from the pro rata share of value of 100% of an equity

interest in a business to reflect the absence of some or all of the powers of control.

- **Majority Control**—The degree of control provided by a majority position.
- **Majority Interest**—An ownership interest greater than 50% of the voting interest in a business enterprise.
- **Minority Discount**—A discount for lack of control applicable to a minority interest.
- **Minority Interest**—An ownership interest less than 50% of the voting interest in a business enterprise.

The definitions provided above include both premium and discount, as well as majority and minority interests. As noted above in the discussion resulting from the spectrum of levels of value, control premiums do, in fact, exist. I have chosen to focus on the discounts associated with control. That decision is a reflection of what I believe you will encounter in the majority of matrimonial litigation cases in North Carolina.

As you can see from the definitions above, a discount for lack of control is a reduction in the value of a 100% interest in the company.[93] This is necessary to reflect the depressed value associated with an interest holder's lack of ability to exercise power or control of the assets of the business enterprise. Jim Hitchner provides a straightforward and simplistic way of understanding this discount, which is to view it through the lens of the minority or non-controlling interest holder. From this perspective, the majority shareholder has the "ability to reduce or eliminate the return on the minority shareholder's investment."[94] To expand on this, these are other elements or aspects of a business that a controlling interest can affect but that a minority interest holder cannot. This list comes from Shannon Pratt's book on discounts and premiums for lack of control and marketability.[95]

- Decide on levels of compensation for officers, directors, and employees
- Decide with whom to do business and enter into binding contracts, including contracts with related parties
- Decide whether to pay dividends and, if so, how much
- Register the stock with the Securities and Exchange Commission for a public offering
- Repurchase outstanding stock or issue new shares
- Make acquisitions or divest subsidiaries or divisions
- Buy, sell, or hypothecate any or all company assets
- Determine capital expenditures
- Change the capital structure
- Amend the articles of incorporation or bylaws
- Sell a controlling interest in the company with or without participation by minority shareholders
- Select directors, officers, and employees
- Determine policy, including changing the direction of the business
- Block any of the above

Consider these two examples where some degree of a discount for lack of control would apply or not apply. In the first example, assume two friends were in business together, owning 67% and 33% of the company, respectively. From inception, the two owners had operated without dissension or opposition. They were both employees of the company and fairly compensated. The majority owner did not run personal expenses through the company. Additionally, the company operated at a profit and those profits were distributed pro-rata to the two owners annually. The 67% owner listened to the other owner though she had the ultimate say in the direction and operations of the company.

For the second example, assume that the minority owner died and her interest transferred to her spouse. Further assume that the majority owner and new minority owner do not get along at all. The majority owner increased her own compensation to an unreasonably high amount and reduced the compensation of the new minority owner to an unreasonably low amount. Further, assume that the company rented the facility that it operated out of from a separate company that was wholly owned by the majority owner. After the transition of the minority ownership, the majority owner increased rent such that there were no profits left to distribute at the end of the year.[96]

In both of these examples, ask yourself the questions: does a discount for lack of control apply? And if so, a low or high discount? The examples are intended to represent opposite ends of a spectrum. The first example may require a discount for lack of control, but not a large discount. Conversely, the second example will require a discount for control, and likely a significant one.

What have the courts said? Unfortunately, at the time of writing this book, there is no clear North Carolina equitable distribution case law on the matter. As we discussed in the Standards of Value chapter, the *Poore v. Poore* case does reference market value. Fair market value is the standard of value identified in every business valuation report I have read for equitable distribution in North Carolina. Fair market value is a standard of value under the value in exchange premise. Meaning, what is the value in the open market, instead of what the value of a company is to the current owner or a specific owner. This leads me to believe that discounts for lack of control apply in North Carolina equitable distribution matters. Those discounts should be tailored to each business valuation assignment. Returning to the example above, if a valuation analyst were to prepare a valuation report with the same discount for each example listed above, I can say that would be wrong. Each discount should be unique to the particular engagement.

There are three tools to assist in estimating what the appropriate discount for lack of control should be. These three tools are to be employed along with the analyst's judgement and experience in concluding on the appropriate discount. Additionally, there might be certain contexts or valuation settings when one or more of the tools is or is not appropriate. The first tool (in no particular order) is a quantitative method comparing the differences in unadjusted and adjusted cash flows. In a previous chapter on normalization adjustments I discussed the different types of adjustments. One type of adjustment listed was a "control adjustment." These adjustments are needed where the controlling owner is using the company to pay excess expenses. Two common examples are owner compensation and related party rent. The value of the company can be different due to the control exerted by the majority owner. I have illustrated this below through a simple example.

Figure 12.3 - Illustrative Example of Differing Conclusions Based on Application of Discounts	
Control Normalization Adjustments:	
Excess Owner/Officer Compensation	35,000
Excess Rent	40,000
Total of Control Adjustments	75,000
Capitalization Rate	15%
Capitalized Effect of Control Adjustments, Rounded	500,000
Minority Value (includes excess compensation and rent)	3,000,000
Effect of Control Adjustments	500,000
Control Value (excludes excess compensation and rent)	3,500,000
Implied Discount for Lack of Control	14%

In the example above, a controlling owner was paying himself amounts in excess of reasonable amounts for compensation and rent. This decision reduces the earnings and the ultimate value of the company. However, if the owner paid reasonable amounts, the expenses would decrease and ultimate value of the company increase. That difference in value between the minority value of $3 million and control value of $3.5 million represents an implied discount for lack of control of 14%. The obvious benefit of utilizing this tool to aid in the final determination of the discount is that it is mathematical and understandable. Occasionally, valuation reports will include several boilerplate pages explaining the need for a discount, or why it applies in a particular instance, and then spring the discount on the reader of the report. The final determination does not seem to be based on any particular facts or figures. That does not mean the stated discount is inaccurate, but the presentation and support for the determination is lacking. The drawback from relying solely on this tool is the unknown—does the 14% in the above example address all of the potentially applicable elements of lack of control noted above?

The next tool available to business valuators is empirical data from the *Mergerstat/BVR Control Premium Study*[97]. This publication compiles the changes in share prices before and after a controlling interest (50.01%) in a security is acquired. In a scenario such as this, an investor is typically willing to pay a premium to acquire a controlling interest. Accordingly, the difference between the price paid for the controlling interest and the value before announcement of the acquisition represents the control premium. This premium can be used to understand the relationship between control value and minority value, and the discount for lack of control. In addition to tracking the fair market value of the security before the announcement that a controlling interest will be acquired, this group compiles the FMV at other intervals between the announcement date and purchase date. Figure 12.4 on the next page is an example of information that is compiled by this publication. In this example, the stock price of a hypothetical security increases by $25.25. This represents a 37.4% premium paid for control over the $67.50 share price prior to the announcement of the acquisition. It also represents a 27.2% discount from the control value for lack of control.

Figure 12.4 - Illustrative Example of Information from *Mergerstat/BVR Control Premium Study*		
Fair market value of shares before announcement	$	67.50
Purchase price of shares	$	92.75
Premium paid for control	$	25.25
Implied control premium		37.4%
Implied discount for lack of control		27.2%

As with the first tool, the obvious benefit is that the results from this publication are not arbitrary since the discount is based upon empirical data. An additional benefit is that the data can be segregated and filtered to match the valuation of a subject company. The resource is more than 20 years old, has catalogued more than 10,000 transactions, and is widely used by valuation analysts, thus supporting its use as a tool in making the determination on the discount for control.

The concerns with using this data are as follows. First, is the fair market value of the stock prior to announcement really what is captured or reported? Or, were there rumors or information garnered from the proverbial "tea leaves" that led to an increase in the stock price prior to the official announcement? Second, while the publication tries to list transactions by type (horizontal integration, vertical integration, conglomerate, or financial) we can never know for certain what role synergies played in the acquisition price. This tool, like so many available to the analyst, needs to be used carefully and consistently.

The final tool is the discount from net asset value data that is available. This tool is used less frequently than the first two and is utilized primarily in asset holding companies. These companies primarily hold real estate, securities, and other investments. There are markets where companies such as these trade. The trading price compared to the net asset value (total assets less total liabilities) represents a discount. See the figure below for a simple example where a 5% interest was acquired for $425,000 in a company with a net asset value of $10 million.

Figure 12.5 - Illustrative Example of Discount from Net Asset Value		
Net Asset Value	$	10,000,000
Interest Acquired		5%
Subtotal	$	500,000
Acquisition Price	$	425,000
Implied Discount		15%

The sources of information for these discounts come from Real Estate Investment Trust (REIT) transactions compiled by various organizations. Partnership Profiles is one organization that compiles discounts of REITs as well as of publicly traded partnerships and closed-end funds. As with the first two tools, great care must be taken in using this data—it must be coupled with the analyst's experience.

DISCOUNTS FOR LACK OF MARKETABILITY

This topic is fraught with difficulties including, but not limited to: what should be included in an understanding of the discounts, sources of data for determination of an appropriate discount, and whether discounts for marketability apply when valuing a controlling interest. The DLOM "more often than not, is the largest dollar discount factor in the valuation of a business interest, particularly a minority interest."[98] My approach with the DLOM will be similar to the DLOC. First, I will provide pertinent definitions and supplement them with a brief discussion, then introduce the attributes of marketability that the analyst has to consider, followed by considerations for North Carolina matrimonial litigators, and sources of information or tools at the analyst's disposal in reaching a determination of an appropriate discount for lack of marketability. First, see below for the pertinent definitions:[99]

- **Discount for Lack of Marketability (Marketability Discount)**—An amount or percentage deducted from the value of an ownership interest to reflect the relative absence of marketability/liquidity.

- **Liquidity**—The ability to quickly convert property to cash.
- **Marketability**—The ability to quickly convert property to cash at minimal cost.

In his book on discounts and premiums, the late Shannon Pratt explained the concept of marketability discounts well. Pratt states:

> "U.S. equity markets are the benchmark for marketability: sell your stock instantly over the phone, at or very close to a known public price, and receive cash in your pocket within three business days. Anything short of that standard of liquidity forms the basis for a discount for lack of marketability. Investors love liquidity and are willing to pay a high premium for it. Conversely, relative to otherwise similar highly liquid securities, investors demand a high discount for lack of liquidity. The market price differential between otherwise comparable, readily marketable and unmarketable interests is greater than most people realize"[100]

Gary Trugman, another well-known business valuator, adds about the DLOM:

> "[I]t is intended to reflect the market's perceived reduction in value for not providing liquidity to the shareholder. Also, it is important to understand that liquidity is not an on-off switch where you either have it or you do not. Rather, liquidity is a continuum where there are varying degrees of liquidity in both the public market and for private companies."[101]

It is likely that you noticed a seemingly important word in those two long quotes (besides marketability) and that was liquidity. Marketability and liquidity are often thought about together. The discount for lack of marketability is theoretically addressing the diminution in value due to a lack of the ability to produce cash from the investment in three days or a short period of time. Consider an example: you own shares of Ford Motor Company, a minority interest in a lawn care business, and a controlling interest in a retail business. The shares in Ford can be converted to cash within three days. The minority interest in the lawn care business most likely precludes you from forcing a sale or taking the company to market, thus a discount would apply. For the controlling interest in the retail business, [102] while you can take the company to market, the market is not as mature and complete as the market for Ford Motor Company shares, and it could take 6-9 months to find a buyer and receive the cash from the sale.

There are many factors that analysts consider when making a determination of the appropriate DLOM. As noted above, there is a spectrum or continuum where illiquidity and lack of marketability can exist. A list of factors for the analyst to consider, though not exhaustive, is as follows:[103]

- Financial statement analysis
- Size and strength of the company
- Size of potential market of buyers
- Costs associated with going public or being acquired
- Dividend / distribution policy
- Nature of the company (history, position in the industry, economic outlook)
- Company's management
- Degree of control in the transferred shares
- Restrictions on transferability of stock
- The holding period for the stock
- Company's redemption policy

Now that we have introduced the concept of the DLOM, let us consider what the courts and general statutes in North Carolina have to say on the matter. If you recall from the chapter on standards, the North Carolina general statutes reference "net value." That is not a standard of value that readily comports to any established standard of value available to the valuation community. Through the *Walter v. Walter* case which references "market value," business valuators understand this to mean "fair market value" and regularly use that as the standard of value in valuation assignments. This is important to note as FMV is a value in exchange. This means that analyst must determine what the business is worth in the open market with hypothetical buyers and sellers. This means that discounts for marketability must be considered. The courts generally have allowed DLOMs for minority interests, and in some cases for controlling interests (i.e., *Crowder v. Crowder*). The *Crowder v. Crowder* case was heard by the NC Appellate Court. The valuation analyst used a DLOM, which was accepted at the district court. The DLOM was not the issue causing the case to be appealed; however, on appeal, the court did not reverse the district court's acceptance of a DLOM for a controlling interest. This does not provide a free pass for DLOMs on controlling interests in North Carolina matrimonial litigation, but should be considered.

Much like discounts for control, the valuator must make a determination of a discount for lack of marketability based upon tools available to them. There are two primary types of empirical studies that are commonly used to support discounts for lack of marketability of minority interests—*restricted stock studies and pre-IPO studies*. In order to understand restricted stock studies, we first need to understand what restricted stock is. Restricted stock arises when a company is first going public or trying to raise capital and does not want the new shareholders to sell off their shares, which could drive the price downward. These issued shares cannot be sold for a certain time and are not registered for public trading. While shareholders cannot exchange these shares on an open market there is a private market for the shares. The restricted stock studies compare the share prices of a particular security on the open market and private market. The price on the open market will almost always exceed the price on the private market because of the ability to be traded freely whenever the holder desires. There have been many studies reviewing transactions over the past 50 years. Reviewing each of these studies is beyond the scope of this chapter. The valuation analyst should read and understand each of the studies that they use to make their determination of the appropriate DLOM.

The other type of empirical study are pre-IPO studies. These studies cataloged data from companies that completed the IPO process. They compared transaction data before a company went public with the public offering price. Typically, the private transaction price was lower thus reflecting a discount.

In addition to the *restricted stock studies* and *pre-IPO studies,* several additional tools have been created to assist the analyst in developing an appropriate discount for lack of marketability. As with the individual restricted stock studies, it is beyond the scope of this chapter to do a deep dive into each.

One final issue in the discussion of marketability discounts is whether discounts for lack of marketability apply to a controlling interest. Jim Hitchner lists this topic in a list of five issues related to discounts that are undecided in the valuation community.[104] The arguments against a DLOM for a controlling interest are as follows:[105]

- Controlling interests have the authority/ability to take their company to market at any time they desire.

- Controlling owners do not have a liquidity concern while their company is on the market because they have the ability to receive distributions/cash flow from the business.

- There is no empirical evidence supporting or measuring a discount for lack of marketability. The restricted stock studies are for minority interests and not applicable to private controlling interests.

- Some opponents would say in an equitable distribution setting, if FMV is the standard of value, that is the value at a particular date and the analyst should presume that the transaction is occurring at that date, not going to market on that date.

- The opponents would acknowledge that there are almost always costs associated with selling and due to the principles of time value of money, a diminution of value. They would argue that the diminution of value does not result from marketability or liquidity constraints.

The arguments for a DLOM for a controlling interest are as follows:[106]

- Although a controlling owner can take his company to market, the market is not as mature and/or efficient as the NASDAQ, resulting in cash return in being delayed for several months. Stated another way, even if it is conceded that there is no marketability concern, there is a liquidity concern.

- The time horizon from deciding to take a company public and selling it represents illiquidity.

- The costs associated with readying the company for sale represent a reduction in value.

- There are several studies that can support and assist in quantifying a DLOM for a controlling interest.

- Controlling interests in private companies sell for lower multiples than comparable public companies.

These are good arguments on both sides. Shannon Pratt notes in his book that the Tax Court has accepted DLOMs for controlling interests, but is "uneven in its applications" thereof.[107] The reasons that Pratt suggests for this inconsistency apply to the question and issue of whether DLOMs should apply to controlling interests in North Carolina in equitable distribution matters. Pratt's three reasons are as follows:[108]

- "Differences in the facts and circumstances from one case to another, even though the differences may not be fully apparent from the summary of facts included in the written opinion."
- "The quality of the expert testimony presented to the court, especially its direct relevance to the facts and circumstances of the case at hand."
- "Which judge is deciding the case?"

My final comment on the present discussion of the applicability of DLOMs on controlling interests is to briefly introduce an alternative method to apply a DLOM. This alternative method is to increase the company-specific risk premium (this was introduced in Chapter 10—Discount Rate and Capitalization Rates) to give effect for the implied or perceived diminution of value in connection with marketability or liquidity concerns. This method of applying a DLOM is less prevalent in the valuation community. In the event that the analyst elects to use this method, there should be an explanation as to why in his view it was appropriate to combine those elements in lieu of separating the rate of return (cost of equity) and DLOM as is the common practice.

I want to address two final matters: key person discounts and the non-additive nature of DLOCs and DLOMs. Key person discounts are closely related to personal goodwill. I previously mentioned personal goodwill in chapters 4 and 7. Personal goodwill is intangible value associated with a person, be it an officer, owner, or anyone else. This is in contrast to enterprise goodwill which is intangible value associated with the business. Personal goodwill cannot be sold or transferred whereas enterprise goodwill can be sold. Accordingly, a business valuator may choose to apply a key person discount to reflect the difference in the value of the company with and without the "key person" working. I noted in chapter 4, the pre-engagement work and meetings are very important. As a part of that work, the standard of value is determined. Will the standard of value be fair market value, fair value, or investment value? The jurisdiction is key here. What do the state statutes and case law state as to the standard of value? Specifically, for matrimonial litigation in North Carolina, the standard of value is a hybrid, adopting through case law a mix of fair market value and investment value. The *Hamby v Hamby* case is helpful for reference. In short (refer to chapter 4 for a lengthier treatment) the personal goodwill was deemed to be marital property. Accordingly, based on this case, a key person discount is not applicable for matrimonial litigation in North Carolina.

The second item is very simple, but very important. The discounts that we have covered in this chapter are not to be additive. The discounts for lack of control and marketability are separate discounts corresponding with different levels of value. As such, one discount is applied to reflect the differences in two levels of value. In the event that both DLOC and DLOM are applicable, the DLOC should be applied first to reflect the differences in value between a control value and a marketable, minority value. Then, the DLOM should be applied to the marketable minority value to reflect the non-marketable, minority value. I have included a table on the next page to reflect this. The result from applying the discounts in this manner is different than simply adding the two discounts together and applying the total percentage.

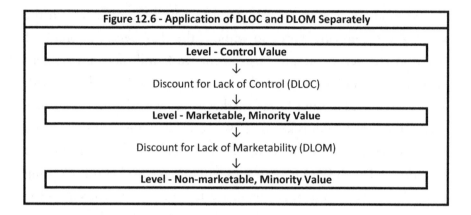

Figure 12.6 - Application of DLOC and DLOM Separately

This chapter introduced the theory of discounts at a basic level to allow you to evaluate the arguments made by the analysts in support of their conclusions on discounts. As you review valuation reports, be aware of seemingly "canned" or boilerplate language supporting the determination. Additionally, look for consistency between other parts of the valuation report and an analyst's determination of discounts. If there is not consistency or if the selection of discounts seems out of place, object and inquire as to why.

This chapter brings to a close a section of this book where I introduced significant topics that warrant lengthy discussion, the individual approaches and discounts to name a few. The next chapter will address several topics that do not warrant a chapter unto themselves, but still important to the ultimate conclusion of value.

CHAPTER 13

MISCELLANEOUS TOPICS

Thus far in this book I have covered many technical subjects that warrant individual consideration. There remain several topics that might seem less significant but still deserve attention for this book to meet its stated goal. Accordingly, I have assembled a short list of topics to briefly cover, preparing you to encounter and engage with them the next time you come across them.

Rain, depending on context, duration, and volume, can have dramatically different effects on and responses from individuals. This reality has always fascinated me. When we have not received rain in some time, we are thankful and delighted to receive its wonderful benefits. When it sprinkles, it can be a nice break in the day and seemingly insignificant. But what is it about rainfall that has undesirable effects? My family spent an extended period of time in Haiti working at an orphanage in 2011. While we were there, I noticed that in some areas most of the trees had been stripped from the land. While there were no doubt benefits from harvesting the trees, there were also subsequent costs. Heavy rains, coupled with other factors, combined to produce mudslides in Haiti, and in other places around the world. Rain can be insignificant, until it is not. Likewise, in business valuation you might not run across any of these issues in the next valuation report you review, but when you do, they could have dramatic effects on the valuation and results in your case.

Non-operating Assets—The first topic we will cover is non-operating assets. These assets are "not necessary to ongoing operations of the business enterprise."[109] What assets does the business not require to produce its profits? The flip side is: what assets can be reasonably argued to be integral to the production of income for the business, and not only this business, but other businesses in this industry? Examples of non-operating assets include but are not limited to the following:

- **Vehicles**—The owner might have purchased one or more vehicles through the company. In many instances, it is reasonable for the officer (who is often the owner) to have the company provide a vehicle for her use. However, it is less likely that she needs multiple vehicles. Further, a vehicle purchased by the business and used by a spouse, child, or other related party is likely a non-operating asset.

- **Real Estate**—Businesses from time to time acquire real estate. The reasons for owning real estate vary but usually are connected to the owner's desire to own the building they occupy in or use the capital available from the business to acquire real estate as an investment. In both cases, these assets are not central to the production of income and thus need to be considered non-operating assets. This is because the realty can be rented, and does not have to be owned.

- **Other Investments**—Similar to the previous example, a business may use the capital available in the business to acquire investments. Depending on the business, there might be a need to have a reasonable amount of stored capital within the company. The officers of the company may elect to store some of that capital as investments in lieu of cash. In those instances it might be reasonable. However, absent a need such as that, the investment is not integral to the operations of the business and should be reflected as a non-operating asset. Common investments are marketable securities and investment land.

There are more instances of non-operating assets but hopefully these three examples illustrate the need for consideration and adjustment. Once the analyst has identified them, she has to determine their fair market value. Much like the asset approach, the analyst will need the help of management, appraisals, or some other source to make that determination. Once the fair market value is known, the analyst will add the fair market value of those assets to the resulting value from the income and market approaches. Since these approaches are valuing only the operating assets of the company, the non-operating assets will have to be added to the indicated value of operations to arrive at the total value for the company. We have included an example in Figure 13.1 to illustrate the effect of non-operating assets on the value of the subject company.

Excess Assets—Excess assets are similar to non-operating assets. These are assets that the valuation analyst has determined to be in excess of what is required to produce the profits or cash flow of the business. Excess assets typically result from having more cash or working capital than deemed necessary for operations. For example, assume that a company had $1 million in cash, $200,000 in accounts receivable, and $150,000 in accounts payable. Those figures would result in working capital of $1,050,000. After looking at the historic balance sheets, historic working capital, historic income statements, and industry comparable financial statements, the analyst determined that a reasonable working capital total was $550,000. In this example, there would be an excess working capital amount of $500,000—more than the company needs. In this example, the $500,000 would be added to the value from the income approach to arrive at the total value of the company. See the example below of how the excess assets of a subject company affect the overall value through the income and market approaches.

Figure 13.1 - Example of Application of Non-operating and Excess Assets		
	Income Approach	Market Approach
Indicated Value (after any applicable discounts for lack of control and or marketability)	1,075,000	1,215,000
Non-operating Assets	45,000	45,000
Excess Assets	500,000	500,000
Total Value, per approach	1,620,000	1,760,000

Reconciliation of Values—The inclusion of this topic may be surprising to you, and I understand why. The phrase "reconciliation of values or approaches" refers to how appraisers weight or use the values from the three different valuation approaches. The example immediately above illustrates this point as well. In that example, the analyst might be inclined to simply average the two approaches to arrive at a conclusion of value for the company of $1,690,000. However, based upon the work she had performed, she might conclude that the income approach was a better indicator and weight it 75% and the market approach 25%, resulting in a conclusion of value for the company of $1,655,000. Absent facts to the contrary, it could be reasonable for the analyst to use either weighting. Appraisers should have a reason, and should disclose that reason for their weighting.

Thus far, this should seem fairly straight forward. But there are two potential issues or cautions I want to mention. First, what happens when the income and market approaches vary significantly? For example, assume a valuation you reviewed reflected a value of $700,000 for the income approach and $2,200,000 for the market approach. In that scenario, it would be hard to argue successfully that using both values was reasonable. Those two values do not reflect two approaches to value a single company, rather, they reflect two different companies or two different scenarios for the subject company. In the event that the analyst did indeed arrive at these two values, instead of averaging them together, she should investigate what lead to the dramatic difference. The benefit stream or discount rate might need to be adjusted. Or, perhaps a different market multiple needs to be selected. This is not to say that the results have to be the same, or that the analyst manipulates figures to get the results close to each other. It is saying that both methods cannot be correct, and one, or possibly both, might be incorrect.

The second potential issue or caution is against using a very low weighting for a particular approach—for instance something less than 20%. Sometimes the analyst will feel an impulse or need to use both approaches but likes or prefers one over the other. Thus, she gives one approach an insignificant weighting. If she does not have more than 20% confidence in one approach then she should likely not weight it all.

Pass-through Entity (PTE) Premium—This topic is one at the center of much discussion, though less recently so for reasons we will present below. This premium is an adjustment to the conclusion of value of a partnership or S-corporation resulting from the perceived benefit associated with the business not having to pay income taxes. A PTE does not pay income taxes because its net profits are passed through to the owner's personal tax return to be taxed. This results in fewer total taxes being paid when compared to a C-corporation that pays taxes, followed by the owner paying a second level of taxes when she receives dividends from the corporation. Thus, it can be argued that an adjustment is required to reflect the premium associated with the additional cash flows that a PTE and its owners receive (by paying less taxes).

Opponents of applying a PTE premium cite the following reasons: lack of convincing empirical studies to support the premium, and the willing buyer concept. There are two studies attempting to support or reject the existence of the PTE premium. The first study was published by Merle Erickson and Shiing-wu Wang in 2002, and concluded that the S corporation premium is approximately 12% to 17%.[110] A second study was published later in 2002 by Michael J. Mattson, Donald S. Shannon, and David E. Upton. The general results of their study were that there was no evidence to support the premium. Their research revealed two factors that are important considerations for this discussion. First, for the largest segment of companies examined, PTEs may sell for a higher amount than a C corporation. The second factor was the inconsistency in the answers to the questions of people interviewed about whether or not they would pay more for an S corporation than a C corporation.[111] The premium might be zero depending on the level of dividends paid, and several other operational aspects of a business.

The second potential objection relates to the willing buyer concept. Simply stated, it is unknown what tax status the acquiring company will be. If analysts must consider a willing buyer or a hypothetical buyer, it is impossible to say with certainty whether the buyer will be a partnership or an S corporation. The buyer will likely choose a tax status that is most beneficial to them. There are many factors to consider when selecting the most beneficial tax status for a particular business.

The PTE premium is a hotly debated topic within the valuation community. There are many well-known valuation analysts that land on both sides of this argument. What I can say is the analyst should be ready to explain her decision to apply or not apply the PTE premium.

This debate was affected by the passage of the tax legislation known as the Tax Cuts and Jobs Act (TCJA) in 2017. This legislation changed the tax rates such that many in the valuation community no longer consider the S corporation premium to exist. Accordingly, the topic is much more of a non-issue for valuations done after the passage of TCJA.[112]

Subsequent Events—The significance of this topic may be better understood in the matrimonial litigation context by using the phrase "known or knowable." The concept and meaning of this phrase is found within the subsequent events section of the standards for business valuation. Paragraph 43 of Statements on Standards for Valuation Services (SSVS) deals with subsequent events. It states:

> The valuation date is the specific date at which the valuation analyst estimates the value of the subject interest and concludes on his or her estimation of value. Generally, the valuation analyst should consider only circumstances existing at the valuation date and events occurring up to the valuation date. An event that could affect the value may occur subsequent to the valuation date; such an occurrence is referred to as a subsequent event. Subsequent events are indicative of conditions that were not *known or knowable* at the valuation date, including conditions that arose subsequent to the valuation date. The valuation would not be updated to reflect those events or conditions. Moreover, the valuation report would typically not include a discussion of those events or conditions because a valuation is performed as of a point in time—the valuation date—and the events described in this subparagraph, occurring subsequent to that date, are not relevant to the value determined as of that date. In situations in which a valuation is meaningful to the intended user beyond the valuation date, the events may be of such nature and significance as to warrant disclosure

(at the option of the valuation analyst) in a separate section of the report in order to keep users informed. Such disclosure should clearly indicate that information regarding the events is provided for information purposes only and does not affect the determination of value as of the specified valuation date.[113]

The notion of a valuation being as of a specific date is extremely important. It is a value as of a particular point, or date. The value of a business might not be significantly different immediately before or after, but it also could be, which underscores the significance of this topic. In preparing a valuation, the analyst can only use information, as the standard says that was "known or knowable at the valuation date." Consider a couple of examples to illustrate the significance. A business in a service industry with a valuation date of December 31, 2020 with a known pending change in government regulation that would negatively impact the company must be considered. Even though the implementation was subsequent to the valuation date, it was known prior to the valuation date. Consider another business with a valuation date of December 31, 2019 that experienced disastrous losses associated with COVID. Should that valuation consider the effects of COVID? Most would argue that it should not. While COVID was beginning to get some attention at the end of 2019, the drastic effects upon the economy and individual businesses were not known or knowable until several months later. Business valuation reports issued towards the end of the first quarter and beyond should consider adding a subsequent event paragraph, but should not adjust their valuation conclusions. Based on this topic alone, determining the date of valuation can have significant effects and results in litigation settings.

Built-in Gains Tax—Another issue in debate among valuators is the built-in gains tax on assets. This issue mainly affects the value determined using the asset approach. When a business is sold, if the sale is structured as an asset sale rather than a stock sale, the business will pay income taxes on the gains realized on its assets. As an example, if a piece of equipment was originally purchased for $100,000, and depreciation was deducted of $60,000 in the years before the sale, it would have a remaining book value of $40,000. If it sold for $70,000 there would be a gain of $30,000 and taxes would be due on this gain. Since valuators are generally valuing a business at fair market value, which is defined as what the business or assets would sell for, should taxes on the sale be deducted as an expense, reducing the asset approach value of the business? Most valuators believe that taxes should be taken into account only if an actual sale is planned or imminent. In this case, the value of the assets at the valuation date should be lower since the business is actually going to have to pay the taxes in the near future, and the cash left for the owner after taxes will be a lower amount. If no sale is planned or imminent, the taxes should probably not be taken into account.

The design of this chapter was to shed some light on several subjects occurring perhaps less frequently than others. Valuation assignments are all different and far from "cookie cutter." Each valuation has at least one nuance, and often more, that makes the assignment both challenging and rewarding. Hopefully, this chapter has helped to expose and explain some of these nuances that make valuations interesting and are capable of producing differing results depending on their treatment.

This chapter marks the end of the introduction of technical subjects related to business valuation. In the next chapter, I introduce common errors in business valuations. Sometimes the errors are just that, errors or mistakes. Other times, unfortunately, the analyst might be guilty of taking too many liberties. Either way, I will take what we learned in previous chapters and highlight some possible errors for you to watch out for.

CHAPTER 14

COMMON ERRORS

The value is what the value is. The charge to the valuation analyst is to develop a conclusion or calculation of value. The result should be unbiased. There are dangers all around the analyst and the respective assignments. However, the analyst must address each of those and deliver, to the best of his ability, an unbiased and supportable conclusion or calculation. The purpose of this chapter is to provide a brief summary of the common areas where errors in business valuations can occur.

During the tax compliance and consulting portion of my career, I often said, "Small mistakes with big numbers equal big mistakes." I am not certain if I coined the phrase or not, but it holds true. The same holds true in business valuation as well, perhaps even more so. The reason why lies in the mathematics within business valuations. Think back to how many times we have discussed in this book factors, multiples, multipliers, formulas, and more. With each of those, a magnification of figures is happening. Therefore, a subtle error, intentional or not, can lead to significant differences in the conclusion of value.

You may have read a valuation report and thought to yourself, "That just does not seem correct." Or perhaps you were involved in a matter where there were two valuations of the same company as of the same date, and the conclusions were significantly different. It is possible that an error occurred in the development of the valuation procedures resulting in a conclusion that is not reasonable. Jim Hitchner, a nationally known business valuator, has presented on this subject several times, often entitling his presentations "How to Detect and Attack a 'Rigged' Valuation—Preparing the Case Against an Unethical Valuation."[114] This chapter will list and briefly discuss the more common areas where errors can occur. Finally, we want to note and make clear that experts can and often do disagree, leading to different conclusions. In an ideal situation, those differences are not significant and can be boiled down to one or two issues.

Benefits—In the chapter on the income approach I introduced this formula:

$$\text{Value} \quad = \quad \frac{\text{Benefits}}{\text{Rate of Return}}$$

I explained that the value of the company resulting from the income approach was represented in this simple formula—future benefits divided by a desired rate of return commensurate to the benefits received. Many, or most, valuations use the income approach alone or in part in conjunction with other methods. Accordingly, it should not come as a shock that these two areas, benefits and return are ripe for errors and "leaning the conclusion" one way or the other. It does not take a rocket scientist to understand the immediate impact to the conclusion of value if the numerator in the formula is changed. In general, the user of a valuation report needs to know the significant effects that can result from changing this figure. Specifically, there are two areas for us to examine that affect the numerator: benefit stream and normalization adjustments.

Benefit Stream—The benefit stream is the valuator's selection of the profits or cash flows of the subject company that are expected to continue into the future. Is the figure reasonable to you, the reader? If you were to purchase the company, based on everything you read in the report, is it reasonable? Inevitably, there will be pages and pages of words, but do you think this company can produce that level of earnings or cash flows into the future? If not, dig deeper. Watch out for a couple of things in that process. How did the analyst weight the historical periods? Did he use a simple average when there appeared to be a trend in revenue and profitability? Did he use the more profitable or less profitable years seemingly without reason and against logic to support a wrong conclusion? If he used cash flows, did he discuss and assign an appropriate capital expenditure required to produce future cash flows? Put a different way, what amount of depreciable assets will be required to produce the expected cash flow? Is that represented in the adjustments to cash flows?

Normalization Adjustments—Another area to pay close attention to is normalization adjustments. This is a significant area in the development of the conclusion, and fertile ground for errors to occur. As a reader of the report, pay attention to or watch out for inconsistencies in the adjustments, or perhaps adjustments all going in one direction or the other, making earnings/cash flows higher or lower. Additionally, watch out for adjustments that seem to contradict other portions of the report. For example, if the officer owner is made out to be in the top 10% in their industry, you should expect their compensation to trend the same way, in the top 10th percentile.

Discount Rate and Capitalization Rate—The second part to the simple formula above is the denominator, the rate of return. This is commonly understood as the required rate of return of an investor associated with a particular stream of future benefits. Subtle changes to the discount rate can lead to substantial differences in the value of a company. There are many different elements that are considered in determining the discount rate. The list from our chapter on discount rates includes the following: risk-free rate, equity risk premium, size premium, industry risk premium, company-specific premium, and beta. Additionally, the growth rate is a significant part of the discussion as well, since the discount rate less the growth rate results in the capitalization rate. At this point I do not need to rehash what was covered in a previous chapter. I will, however, address possible or common errors for several elements of the discount rate and capitalization rate.

- **Equity Risk Premium**—Based on the amount of data available to the valuator, this figure should be in the range of 4% to 7%. Anything outside this range is questionable and should be explained well.[115]

- **Size Premium**—Many valuation reports may be for companies that are very small, and thus have a higher required rate of return. Kroll Cost of Capital has attempted to measure that additional required rate of return by dividing their data into 10 deciles.[116] Since even the 10th decile represents companies larger than most of the companies that you will read about in valuation reports, the 10th decile was divided into separate groups: 10a and 10b. Further, 10a was divided to 10w and 10x; and 10b to 10y and 10z. Many valuation analysts prefer to use the 10th decile based on many informal polls. The use of 10z information should be used sparingly as it includes data of distressed companies and results in a very high discount rate.

- **Industry Risk Premium**—The industry risk premium, in theory, is a good addition to the discount rate. It can be negative or positive, to reflect the inherent riskiness of the subject industry to that of the average represented in all industries. Beware of large premiums, either positive or negative. Also, ask yourself the question, does this make sense and is it consistent with the rest of the report?

- **Company-Specific Premium**—This premium, more so than any other, is where errors can occur. The other elements of risk and return are based on historic data that is widely known, and accepted. This element is not based on empirical data, but on the judgement of the analyst in consideration of all factors. It has been said that business valuation is an art and a science. Fortunately, and thankfully, through the dedication of many to this field, there is now more science to it than ever before. Yet, the determination of the company-specific premium remains perhaps the most "art" of any part of a business valuation.

- **Growth Rate**—The common error with the determination of the growth rate is that it is either too high or too low. The growth rate is intended to represent the long-term growth rate into perpetuity, not for just the next 5 or 10 years. Accordingly, using a growth rate in excess of 7%, for example, to capitalize earnings or cash flow would likely be suspect. What investment is going to grow at that rate and significantly more than the historical market? On the other side of the coin, valuators can assign a growth rate too low. If we were to assume that ongoing inflation is 2.5% and the valuation analyst assigns a growth rate of 2.5% then he is essentially saying there will be no real growth. The selection of the long-term growth rate should be the nominal growth rate. The nominal growth rate is the real growth rate plus inflation.

Failure to Reconcile Approaches—Another possible error in valuations includes the failure to reconcile the approaches. Ideally, the different approaches should result in similar values, or at least for the income and market approaches. If the analyst provides the values from two different approaches, and the results are vastly different than there is either an error or a plausible reason for the difference. For example, assume the income approach and market approaches produce values of $500,000 and $1,500,000, respectively. These values, as is, cannot both be correct and most likely should not be averaged together to produce a $1,000,000 value. Instead, the analyst should investigate each for potential errors in the development of their approaches.

Market Approach—The market approach can be a significant part of the analyst's conclusion of value. It can also be the source of errors and mistakes. The primary errors and or mistakes are less than adequate sample size and using the incorrect multiples. First, does the sample of completed transactions reflect the company? Of course, they will not be an exact replica, they cannot be—they are different companies. Are there enough companies to create a consensus that companies sell for a particular multiple or factor? Specific errors in the selection of companies could be as follows (though not an exhaustive list): too few companies to be considered a reasonable sample, revenue that is much higher or lower than the subject company, and selection of companies that are clearly outside the norm producing exponentially higher multiples. Second, once the selection of companies has been made, what multiples does the analyst use to apply to the subject company to result in a value? The median could be used and often is, or perhaps the mean, the 75th and 90th percentile, or moving in the other direction, the 25th or 10th percentile.

Users of business valuations need to take their role seriously. Of course, there is going to be a certain level of confidence with and reliance upon the analyst or else you would not be working with him.

Your review of the report should be welcomed by the analyst and seen as an opportunity to strengthen the report. As you read, review, and use the report, bring with you your knowledge of the business, common sense, and all that you know about business valuations. Further, do not hesitate to ask about an assumption, adjustment, or determination in the report. Each and every position in the report should be supportable and have a foundation.

ACKNOWLEDGMENTS

There are many people who have contributed in both big and small ways to bring this book to life. I'd like to take this opportunity to acknowledge a few of them.

First of all, I want to thank Carr, Riggs & Ingram, my partners, and my friends. Thank you for all the opportunities, encouragement, and support in my career and this book. You have been gracious to me in ways in which I do not deserve.

A special thanks to Hank Crawford, my mentor and more importantly my friend. The lessons in business valuation, business in general, and in life are immeasurable. I can humbly and honestly say I would not be at this point without you.

And to Rod Burkert, "I think you should write a book" you said. Here we are two years later. Your guidance, proverbial shoves, and accountability were necessary for this project and my practice. Thank you!

Last, and certainly not least, thank you to my family. Kalea, Luke, Abigail, Judson & Elliot—I love you. This book would not be possible without your patience and support. For all the times that I asked you to be quiet while on a call or rushed you out of my office, apologies and thank you. I count being your father one of the greatest blessings of my life. I love you! Meme and Papa—you gave and continue to give so much of yourselves to me. Accordingly, all that I do finds threads, traces and roots in you and my relationship as your son.

ENDNOTES

1.   National Association of Certified Valuators and Analysts. "International Glossary of Business Valuation Terms." International Glossary of Business Valuation Terms, June 8, 2001. https://nacva.com/glossary.

2.   National Association of Certified Valuators and Analysts. "International Glossary of Business Valuation Terms." International Glossary of Business Valuation Terms, June 8, 2001. https://www.nacva.com/glossary#terms_F.

3.   National Association of Certified Valuators and Analysts. "International Glossary of Business Valuation Terms." International Glossary of Business Valuation Terms, June 8, 2001. https://www.nacva.com/glossary#terms_i.

4.   Financial Accounting Standards Board (FASB). "820 Fair Value Measurement." Accounting Standards Codification (ASC) Topic 820, https://asc.fasb.org/820/tableOfContent.

5.   National Association of Certified Valuators and Analysts. "International Glossary of Business Valuation Terms." International Glossary of Business Valuation Terms, June 8, 2001. https://www.nacva.com/glossary#terms_i.

6. National Association of Certified Valuators and Analysts. "International Glossary of Business Valuation Terms." International Glossary of Business Valuation Terms, June 8, 2001. https://www. nacva.com/glossary#terms_G.

7. National Association of Certified Valuators and Analysts. "International Glossary of Business Valuation Terms." International Glossary of Business Valuation Terms, June 8, 2001. https://www. nacva.com/glossary#terms_L.

8. Cornell Law School. Treasury Regulation Section 20.2031-1(b). 26 CFR § 20.2031-1 - Definition of gross estate; valuation of property. | Electronic Code of Federal Regulations (e-CFR) | US Law | LII / Legal Information Institute (cornell.edu).

9. National Association of Certified Valuators and Analysts. "International Glossary of Business Valuation Terms." International Glossary of Business Valuation Terms, June 8, 2001. https://www. nacva.com/glossary#terms_F.

10. National Association of Certified Valuators and Analysts. "International Glossary of Business Valuation Terms." International Glossary of Business Valuation Terms, June 8, 2001. https://www. nacva.com/glossary#terms_i.

11. Jay E. Fishman, Shannon P. Pratt, and William J. Morrison, *Standards of Value: Theory and Applications, 2nd Ed.* (Hoboken: John Wiley & Sons, Inc., 2013), 25.

12. Financial Accounting Standards Board (FASB). "820 Fair Value Measurement." Accounting Standards Codification (ASC) Topic 820, https://asc.fasb.org/820/tableOfContent .

13. *Webster's Third New International Dictionary* (Springfield: G&G Merriam Company, 1966).

14.   Bryan A. Garner, ed., *Black's Law Dictionary, 6th ed.* (New York: West Publishing, 1991), 1587.

15.   Jay E. Fishman, Shannon P. Pratt, and William J. Morrison. *Standards of Value: Theory and Applications, 2nd Ed.* (Hoboken: John Wiley & Sons, Inc.), 20.

16.   Fishman, Pratt, and Morrison. *Standards of Value,* 21.

17.   Bryan A. Garner, ed., *Black's Law Dictionary, 6th ed.* (New York: West Publishing, 1991), 1587.

18.   National Association of Certified Valuators and Analysts. "International Glossary of Business Valuation Terms." International Glossary of Business Valuation Terms, June 8, 2001. https://www.nacva.com/glossary#terms_G.

19.   Bryan A. Garner, ed., Black's Law Dictionary, 6th ed. (New York: West Publishing, 1991), 1587.

20.   National Association of Certified Valuators and Analysts. "International Glossary of Business Valuation Terms." International Glossary of Business Valuation Terms, June 8, 2001. https://www.nacva.com/glossary#terms_L.

21.   Shannon P. Pratt and Alina V. Niculita, *Valuing a Business: The Analysis and Appraisal of Closely Held Companies, 5th Ed.* (New York: The McGraw-Hill Companies, Inc., 2008), 47-48.

22.   Jay E. Fishman, Shannon P. Pratt, and William J. Morrison, *Standards of Value: Theory and Applications, 2nd Ed.* (Hoboken: John Wiley & Sons, Inc., 2013), 269, 417, and 418.

23.   N.C. Gen. Stat. § 50-20(c). https://www.ncleg.gov/EnactedLegislation/Statutes/HTML/ByChapter/Chapter_50.html

24.   Hamby v. Hamby, 143 N.C. App. 635, 2001-N.C. App.

25.   Hamby v. Hamby, 143 N.C. App. 635, 2001-N.C. App.

26.   Hamby v. Hamby.

27.   Hamby v. Hamby, 143 N.C. App. 635, 2001-N.C. App.

28.   Hamby v. Hamby.

29.   Poore v. Poore, 75 N.C. App. 414, 331 S.E.2d 266, 1985 N.C. App. LEXIS 3680.

30.   Crowder v. Crowder, 147 N.C. App. 677, 556 S.E. 2d 639, 2001 N.C. App.

31.   Walter v. Walter, 149 N.C. App. 723, 561 S.E.2d 571, 2002 N.C. App LEXIS 290.

32.   Jay E. Fishman, et al. *Standards of Value: Theory and Applications. 2nd Ed.* (Hoboken: John Wiley & Sons, Inc., 2013), 417-418.

33.   This definition includes phrases from definitions of fair market value and investment value provided by the "International Glossary of Business Valuation Terms." International Glossary of Business Valuation Terms, June 8, 2001. https://www.nacva.com/glossary#terms_F and IRS Treasury Regulations Treasury Regulation Section 20.2031-1(b).

34.   AICPA Consulting Services Executive Committee, Statements on Standards for Valuation Services: VS Section 100 (American Institute of Certified Public Accountants, 2007), VS 100, Paragraph 21(a), https://www.aicpa.org/resources/download/statement-on-standards-for-valuation-services-vs-section-100

35.   AICPA Consulting Services Executive Committee, Statements on Standards for Valuation Services: VS Section 100 (American Institute of Certified Public Accountants, 2007), VS 100, Paragraph 21(b) https://www.aicpa.org/resources/download/statement-on-standards-for-valuation-services-vs-section-100

36) AICPA Consulting Services Executive Committee, Statements on Standards for Valuation Services: VS Section 100 (American Institute of Certified Public Accountants, 2007), VS 100, Paragraph 77, https://www.aicpa.org/resources/download/statement-on-standards-for-valuation-services-vs-section-100

37) AICPA Consulting Services Executive Committee, Statements on Standards for Valuation Services: VS Section 100 (American Institute of Certified Public Accountants, 2007), VS 100, Paragraph 21(a), https://www.aicpa.org/resources/download/statement-on-standards-for-valuation-services-vs-section-100

38) AICPA Consulting Services Executive Committee, Statements on Standards for Valuation Services: VS Section 100 (American Institute of Certified Public Accountants, 2007), VS 100, Paragraph 69, https://www.aicpa.org/resources/download/statement-on-standards-for-valuation-services-vs-section-100

39) AICPA Consulting Services Executive Committee, Statements on Standards for Valuation Services: VS Section 100 (American Institute of Certified Public Accountants, 2007), VS 100, Paragraph 21 (b), https://www.aicpa.org/resources/download/statement-on-standards-for-valuation-services-vs-section-100

40) AICPA Consulting Services Executive Committee, Statements on Standards for Valuation Services: VS Section 100 (American Institute of Certified Public Accountants, 2007), VS 100, Paragraph 77, https://www.aicpa.org/resources/download/statement-on-standards-for-valuation-services-vs-section-100

41) AICPA Consulting Services Executive Committee, Statements on Standards for Valuation Services: VS Section 100 (American Institute of Certified Public Accountants, 2007), VS 100, Paragraph 51, https://www.aicpa.org/resources/download/statement-on-standards-for-valuation-services-vs-section-100

42.   AICPA Consulting Services Executive Committee, Statements on Standards for Valuation Services: VS Section 100 (American Institute of Certified Public Accountants, 2007), VS 100, Paragraph 71, https://www.aicpa.org/resources/download/statement-on-standards-for-valuation-services-vs-section-100

43.   AICPA Consulting Services Executive Committee, Statements on Standards for Valuation Services: VS Section 100 (American Institute of Certified Public Accountants, 2007), VS 100, Paragraph 78 https://www.aicpa.org/resources/download/statement-on-standards-for-valuation-services-vs-section-100

44.   AICPA Consulting Services Executive Committee, Statements on Standards for Valuation Services: VS Section 100 (American Institute of Certified Public Accountants, 2007), VS 100, Paragraph 50, https://www.aicpa.org/resources/download/statement-on-standards-for-valuation-services-vs-section-100

45.   "Health Supplement Stores," First Research Industry Profile database, accessed 2022, Industry Statistics, Trends and Analysis from First Research, a D&B Company.

46.   AICPA Consulting Services Executive Committee, Statements on Standards for Valuation Services: VS Section 100 (American Institute of Certified Public Accountants, 2007), VS 100, Paragraph 27, https://www.aicpa.org/resources/download/statement-on-standards-for-valuation-services-vs-section-100

47.   James R. Hitchner, *Financial Valuation: Applications and Models. 3rd Ed.* (Hoboken: John Wiley & Sons, Inc., 2011), 64-65.

48.   AICPA Consulting Services Executive Committee, Statements on Standards for Valuation Services: VS Section 100 (American Institute of Certified Public Accountants, 2007), VS 100, Paragraph 27, https://www.aicpa.org/resources/download/statement-on-standards-for-valuation-services-vs-section-100

49.   Frank K. Reilly, *Investment Analysis and Portfolio Management, 7th ed.* (Mason: South-Western, 2003), 374.

50.   James R. Hitchner, *Financial Valuation: Applications and Models, 3rd ed.* (Hoboken: John Wiley & Sons, Inc., 2011), 121-122.

51.   Shannon P. Pratt and Alina V. Niculita. *Valuing a Business: The Analysis and Appraisal of Closely Held Companies, 5th ed.* (New York: The McGraw-Hill Companies, Inc., 2008), 181.

52.   James R. Hitchner, *Financial Valuation: Applications and Models, 3rd ed.* (Hoboken: John Wiley & Sons, Inc., 2011), 122-123.

53.   James R. Hitchner, "How to detect and Attack a Rigged Valuation – Preparing the Case Against an Unethical Valuation." Lecture, AICPA conference, Las Vegas, NV, November 14, 2017.

54.   James R. Hitchner, *Financial Valuation: Applications and Models, 3rd ed.* (Hoboken: John Wiley & Sons, Inc., 2011), 131.

55.   Gary R. Trugman, *Understanding Business Valuation: A Practical Guide to Valuing Small to Medium Sized Business, 5th Ed.* (Hoboken: John Wiley & Sons, 2017), 479.

56.   Trugman, 480.

57.   James R. Hitchner, *Financial Valuation: Applications and Models, 3rd ed.* (Hoboken: John Wiley & Sons, Inc., 2011), 134.

58.   Hitchner, 134.

59.   National Association of Certified Valuators and Analysts. Training Material. (2012 version) Chapter 4, page 13.

60.   National Association of Certified Valuators and Analysts. "International Glossary of Business Valuation Terms." International Glossary of Business Valuation Terms, June 8, 2001. https://nacva. com/glossary#terms_C. Accessed on 2/16/22.

61.   James R. Hitchner, *Financial Valuation: Applications and Models, 3rd ed.* (Hoboken: John Wiley & Sons, Inc., 2011), 140; Shannon P. Pratt and Alina V. Niculita. *Valuing a Business: The Analysis and Appraisal of Closely Held Companies, 5th ed.* (New York: The McGraw-Hill Companies, Inc., 2008), 239-241.

62.   National Association of Certified Valuators and Analysts. "International Glossary of Business Valuation Terms." International Glossary of Business Valuation Terms, June 8, 2001, https://www.nacva.com/glossary#terms_D. Accessed on February 16, 2022.

63.   Shannon P. Pratt and Alina V. Niculita. *Valuing a Business: The Analysis and Appraisal of Closely Held Companies, 5th ed.* (New York: The McGraw-Hill Companies, Inc., 2008), 177.

64.   Pratt and Niculita, 177.

65.   James R. Hitchner, *Financial Valuation: Applications and Models, 3rd ed.* (Hoboken: John Wiley & Sons, Inc., 2011), 143-145.

66.   National Association of Certified Valuators and Analysts. "International Glossary of Business Valuation Terms." International Glossary of Business Valuation Terms, June 8, 2001, https://www.nacva.com/glossary#terms_T. Accessed on February 18, 2022.

67.   IRS Revenue Ruling 68-609; *James R. Hitchner, Financial Valuation: Applications and Models, 3rd ed.* (Hoboken: John Wiley & Sons, Inc., 2011), 159.

68.   National Association of Certified Valuators and Analysts. "International Glossary of Business Valuation Terms." International Glossary of Business Valuation Terms, June 8, 2001, https://www.nacva.com/glossary#terms_E. Accessed on February 18, 2022.

69.   National Association of Certified Valuators and Analysts, https://www.nacva.com/glossary#terms_E. Accessed on February 18, 2022.

70.	Format for this figure came from the business valuation software, ValuSource Pro.

71.	James R. Hitchner, *Financial Valuation: Applications and Models, 3rd ed.* (Hoboken: John Wiley & Sons, Inc., 2011), 124.

72.	Hitchner, 124, and Gregory R. Caruso, *The Art of Business Valuation: Accurately Valuing a Small Business* (Hoboken: John Wiley & Sons, Inc., 2020), 82.

73.	James R. Hitchner, *Financial Valuation: Applications and Models, 3rd ed.* (Hoboken: John Wiley & Sons, Inc., 2011), 125; Gregory R. Caruso, *The Art of Business Valuation: Accurately Valuing a Small Business* (Hoboken: John Wiley & Sons, Inc., 2020), 91-92.

74.	Included in Alexander F. Chamberlain's book written in 1896. *The Child and Childhood in Folk Thought.* When it was originally coined is unknown.

75.	James R. Hitchner, *Financial Valuation: Applications and Models, 3rd ed.* (Hoboken: John Wiley & Sons, Inc., 2011), 183.

76.	Gary R. Trugman, *Understanding Business Valuation: A Practical Guide to Valuing Small to Medium Sized Business, 5th ed.* (Hoboken: John Wiley & Sons, 2017), 511.

77.	James R. Hitchner, *Financial Valuation: Applications and Models, 3rd ed.* (Hoboken: John Wiley & Sons, Inc., 2011), 183.

78.	Gary R. Trugman, *Understanding Business Valuation: A Practical Guide to Valuing Small to Medium Sized Business, 5th ed.* (Hoboken: John Wiley & Sons, 2017), 361-363.

79.	National Association of Certified Valuators and Analysts. "International Glossary of Business Valuation Terms." International Glossary of Business Valuation Terms, June 8, 2001, https://www.nacva.com/glossary#terms_R. Accessed on March 4, 2022.

80.   National Association of Certified Valuators and Analysts, https://www.nacva.com/glossary#terms_E. Accessed March 4, 2022.

81.   Shannon P. Pratt and Alina V. Niculita. *Valuing a Business: The Analysis and Appraisal of Closely Held Companies, 5th ed.* (New York: The McGraw-Hill Companies, Inc., 2008), 202-203.

82.   National Association of Certified Valuators and Analysts. "International Glossary of Business Valuation Terms." International Glossary of Business Valuation Terms, June 8, 2001, https://www. nacva.com/glossary#terms_B. Accessed on March 4, 2022.

83.   James R. Hitchner, *Financial Valuation: Applications and Models, 3rd ed.* (Hoboken: John Wiley & Sons, Inc., 2011), 1,252.

84.   Gary R. Trugman, *Understanding Business Valuation: A Practical Guide to Valuing Small to Medium Sized Business, 5th ed.* (Hoboken: John Wiley & Sons, 2017), 561-562.

85.   National Association of Certified Valuators and Analysts. "International Glossary of Business Valuation Terms." International Glossary of Business Valuation Terms, June 8, 2001. https://nacva. com/glossary#terms_M. Accessed on March 9, 2022.

86.   National Association of Certified Valuators and Analysts. "International Glossary of Business Valuation Terms." International Glossary of Business Valuation Terms, June 8, 2001. https://nacva. com/glossary#terms_M. Accessed on March 11, 2022.

87.   National Association of Certified Valuators and Analysts. "International Glossary of Business Valuation Terms." International Glossary of Business Valuation Terms, June 8, 2001. https://nacva. com/glossary#terms _G. Accessed on March 11, 2022.

88.   Information available through BIZCOMPS and DealStats™ web-based application, Business Valuation Resources, https://www. bvresources.com/.

89.   The levels of value spectrum presented here is based upon review of several books including the following texts. In addition, it should be noted that some authors and analysts would add a level below control value reflective of publicly traded stock which is non-controlling, yet marketable. James R. Hitchner, *Financial Valuation: Applications and Models, 3rd ed.* (Hoboken: John Wiley & Sons, Inc., 2011), 366-367; Gregory R. Caruso, *The Art of Business Valuation: Accurately Valuing a Small Business* (Hoboken: John Wiley & Sons, Inc., 2020), 223; Shannon Pratt, *Business Valuation Discounts and Premiums, 2nd ed.* (Hoboken: John Wiley & Sons, Inc., 2009), 5.

90.   Shannon Pratt, *Business Valuation Discounts and Premiums, 2nd ed.* (Hoboken: John Wiley & Sons, Inc., 2009), 8-9.

91.   Shannon Pratt, *Business Valuation Discounts and Premiums, 2nd ed.* (Hoboken: John Wiley & Sons, Inc., 2009), 6-7.

92.   National Association of Certified Valuators and Analysts. "International Glossary of Business Valuation Terms." International Glossary of Business Valuation Terms. June 8, 2001. https://www.nacva.com/glossary#terms_D. Accessed on April 5, 2022.

93.   This statement assumes as noted above that the approaches, specifically, the income and market approaches are producing a controlling level of value. See the above discussion for more on this topic.

94.   James R. Hitchner, *Financial Valuation: Applications and Models, 3rd ed.* (Hoboken: John Wiley & Sons, Inc., 2011), 371.

95.   Shannon Pratt, *Business Valuation Discounts and Premiums, 2nd ed.* (Hoboken: John Wiley & Sons, Inc., 2009), 17-18.

96.   Example adapted from an example taken from *The Art of Business Valuation* by Greg Caruso. Gregory R. Caruso, *The Art of*

Business Valuation: Accurately Valuing a Small Business (Hoboken: John Wiley & Sons, Inc., 2020), 238.

97.   FactSet Mergerstat/BVR Control Premium Study is published annually.

98.   Shannon Pratt, *Business Valuation Discounts and Premiums, 2nd ed.* (Hoboken: John Wiley & Sons, Inc., 2009), 86.

99.   National Association of Certified Valuators and Analysts. "International Glossary of Business Valuation Terms." International Glossary of Business Valuation Terms, June 8, 2001. https://nacva.com/glossary#terms_D. Accessed on April 5, 2022.

100.   Shannon Pratt, *Business Valuation Discounts and Premiums, 2nd ed.* (Hoboken: John Wiley & Sons, Inc., 2009), 86-87.

101.   Gary R. Trugman, *Understanding Business Valuation: A Practical Guide to Valuing Small to Medium Sized Business, 5th ed.* (Hoboken: John Wiley & Sons, 2017), 597.

102.   As noted above, this is a topic of much disagreement. The inclusion here is for example purposes and does not represent a position taken as to the appropriateness of a DLOM on a controlling interest.

103.   This list represents a combination of the case commonly referred to as the Mandelbaum Case [Bernard Mandelbaum, et al v. Commissioner of Internal Revenue (T.C. Memo 1995-255, June 12, 1995)] and from Shannon Pratt's book [Shannon Pratt, *Business Valuation Discounts and Premiums, 2nd ed.* (Hoboken: John Wiley & Sons, Inc., 2009), 87].

104.   James R. Hitchner, *Financial Valuation: Applications and Models. 3rd Ed.* (Hoboken: John Wiley & Sons, Inc., 2011), 371.

105.   Hitchner, 381-382; Gary R. Trugman, *Understanding Business Valuation: A Practical Guide to Valuing Small to Medium Sized Business, 5th ed.* (Hoboken: John Wiley & Sons, 2017), 598-599; Shannon P. Pratt and Alina V. Niculita, *Valuing a Business: The Analysis and Appraisal of Closely Held Companies, 5th ed.* (New York: The McGraw-Hill Companies, Inc. 2008), 200-202.

106.   James R. Hitchner, 381-382; Trugman, pages 598-599; Pratt and Niculita, 200-202.

107.   Shannon P. Pratt and Alina V. Niculita, *Valuing a Business: The Analysis and Appraisal of Closely Held Companies, 5th ed.* (New York: The McGraw-Hill Companies, Inc., 2008), 210.

108.   Pratt and Niculita, 210.

109.   National Association of Certified Valuators and Analysts. "International Glossary of Business Valuation Terms." International Glossary of Business Valuation Terms, June 8, 2001. https://www.nacva.com/glossary#terms_N. Accessed on March 15, 2022.

110.   Gary R. Trugman, *Understanding Business Valuation: A Practical Guide to Valuing Small to Medium Sized Business, 5th ed.* (Hoboken: John Wiley & Sons, 2017), 760.

111.   Gary R. Trugman, *Understanding Business Valuation: A Practical Guide to Valuing Small to Medium Sized Business, 5th ed.* (Hoboken: John Wiley & Sons, 2017), 760.

112.   This is a general statement. TCJA did limit a certain newly invented deduction commonly referred to as the Qualified Business Income Deduction to non-service businesses. Accordingly, for those valuation analysts preferring to apply an S corporation premium, TCJA might not affect their application of a premium on certain service businesses.

113.   AICPA Consulting Services Executive Committee, Statements on Standards for Valuation Services: VS Section 100 (American Institute of Certified Public Accountants, 2007), VS 100, Paragraph 43, https://www.aicpa.org/resources/download/statement-on-standards-for-valuation-services-vs-section-100 .

114.   James R. Hitchner, "How to detect and Attack a Rigged Valuation – Preparing the Case Against an Unethical Valuation." Lecture, AICPA conference, Las Vegas, NV, November 14, 2017. Many items on the list below come from him. All of these items are well known to anyone who has prepared business valuations for at least a short period of time.

115.   James R. Hitchner, "How to detect and Attack a Rigged Valuation – Preparing the Case Against an Unethical Valuation." Lecture, AICPA conference, slide 12, Las Vegas, NV, November 14, 2017.

116.   Gary R. Trugman, *Understanding Business Valuation: A Practical Guide to Valuing Small to Medium Sized Business, 5th ed.* (Hoboken: John Wiley & Sons, 2017), 521.

INDEX

Figures and notes are indicated by *f* and *n*, respectively, after the page number.

A

ABV (Accredited in Business Valuation), 28, 29–31
accelerated depreciation, 122–123, 128
accounting methods. *See* generally accepted accounting principles; tax basis accounting
accounts payable adjustments, 89
accounts receivable adjustments, 83–85, 85*f*
accounts receivable turnover ratios, 74
Accredited in Business Valuation (ABV), 28, 29–31
Accredited Senior Appraiser (ASA), 28, 29–31
accrual basis accounting, 83, 85*f*, 122–123
accrued payroll, 89
adjusted book value method
    accounts payable adjustments, 89
    accounts receivable adjustments, 83–85, 85*f*
    cash adjustments, 83
    debt, 89–90
    deferred tax asset/liability, 90
    equipment/furniture, 87
    general discussion, 7, 22, 82, 91*f*
    income tax effects, 90–92
    intangible assets, 7, 88
    inventory adjustments, 85–86
    investment adjustments, 86–87
    land/buildings, 87
    leasehold improvements, 87–88
    other current liabilities, 89
    shareholder loans, 88–89
American Institute of Certified Public Accountants (AICPA), 27–31
American Society of Appraisers (ASA), 7, 27–31

amortization, 128–129
analyses. *See also* company analysis
    common errors, 78
    common size statements, 9, 72–75
    general discussion, 69–70
    industry, 76
    SWOT, 71–75
anticipated capital expenditures adjustments, 102
appraisals. *See* valuations
arbitrage pricing theory, 8
ASA (American Society of Appraisers), 7, 27–31
asset approach
    calculation/valuation engagements, 56–57, 61–62
    general discussion, 8, 22, 79–81, 92
    levels of value spectrum, 152–155, 153*f*, 153*n*
    liquidation value, 82
asset-intensive companies, 80–81
asset risk, 134

B

balance sheet
    asset adjusted book value method
        accounts payable adjustments, 89
        accounts receivable adjustments, 83–85, 85*f*
        cash adjustments, 83
        debt, 89–90
        deferred tax asset/liability, 90
        equipment/furniture, 87
        income tax effects, 90–92
        intangible assets, 7, 88
        inventory adjustments, 85–86
        investment adjustments, 86–87
        land/buildings, 87
        leasehold improvements, 87–88

other current liabilities, 89
  overview, 82, 91*f*
  shareholder loans, 88–89
common size statements, 9, 72–75
general discussion, 22, 79–81, 92
net book value, 15
preparation methods, 82
basic accounting records, 3–4
Beightol v. Beightol, 48–49
benefit stream
  cash flow model, 101–103, 102*f*
  common errors, 182–183
  earnings model, 100–101
  general discussion, 78, 100
  historical financial statements,
  103–108
  normalization adjustments, 100, 101*f*
  risk and, 133–135
  valuation formula
    discount/capitalization rates,
    131–133
    overview, 95–97, 98, 109
beta, 8, 14, 18, 137
BIZCOMPS database, 143, 146*f*, 147
Black's Law Dictionary, 39, 41–42
blockage discount, 8
book basis depreciation, 128
book value, 15, 82
brokers, 27, 142
buildings/land, 87, 172, 173
build-up method (BUM), 138, 140
built-in gains tax on assets, 178–179
business enterprise, 8
business risk, 8, 134
business valuation. *See also* valuations
  basic concepts/general discussion,
  21–23
  credentialing/standards, 27–32
  general discussion, 8
  purpose, 25–27
  terminology, 7–19

C

calculation engagements
  general discussion, 21–23, 55–56
  pre-engagement planning, 66, 67–68

reports
  exception provision, 30–31,
  64–67
  oral, 55, 62, 63–64
  overview, 23, 55
  written, 62–63
valuation
  approaches, 56–57
  expression of results, 58–61
  overview, 61–62
  scope/procedures limitations,
  57–58
calculation of value, 21–23
Canada, 7, 11–12, 13, 16, 19
Canadian Institute of Chartered
  Business Valuators, 7
capital asset pricing model (CAPM),
  8–9
capitalization rate
  calculating, 135–140
  capitalized cash flow method, 110–
  112
  common errors, 183–185
  general discussion, 9, 78, 131–133
  multiples and, 15
  risk and, 133–135
  valuation formula, 131
capitalized cash flow/earnings method,
  22, 99–100, 109–112
capital structure, 9
CAPM (capital asset pricing model),
  8–9
case law, 27, 34, 39, 43–44. *See also*
  North Carolina case law
cash adjustments, 83–85
cash basis, 83, 89, 122, 123–124, 125
cash flow model, 9, 101–103, 102*f*
Certified in Financial Forensics (CFF),
  27, 28
certified public accountants (CPAs),
  27–31
Certified Valuation Analyst (CVA), 28
checklists, 30
clients/customers
  in analyses, 71, 72, 76
  general discussion, 12, 26, 45, 136

COGS (cost of goods sold), 125
collectability, 84–85, 85f
common errors
  in analyses, 78
  benefit stream, 182–183
  capitalization/discount rate, 183–185
  general discussion, 181–182
  income approach, 98–99
  market approach, 186–187
  normalization adjustments, 183
  pre-tax/after-tax benefits, 97
  reconciliation of values/approaches,
    185–186
common size statements, 9, 72–75
company analysis
  common errors, 78
  economic environment analysis,
    76–77
  financial/quantitative data, 72–75
  general discussion, 69–70, 77–78
  industry analysis, 76
  non-financial/qualitative data, 70–72
  ratios chart, 73–75
  SWOT, 71–75
company-specific premium, 3–4, 136–
  137, 168, 185
conclusion of value, 21–23
control
  general discussion, 9, 19. *see also*
    discounts for lack of control
  level value, 152–155, 153f, 153n
  premium, 9–10, 160–161, 161f
control/discretionary adjustments,
  120–121
controlling interests, 44, 51–52, 166–
  168
copyrights, 13. *See also* intangible assets
cost approach, 10
cost of capital
  calculating, 135–140
  capitalized cash flow/earnings
    method, 110–112
  common errors, 183–185
  foundational questions, 34
  general discussion, 10, 131–133
  risk and, 133–135

  valuation formula, 95–97, 98, 131
  WACC, 19, 139–140
cost of goods sold (COGS), 125
COVID-19 pandemic, 77, 105, 122,
  124–125, 178
CPAs (certified public accountants),
  27–31
credentials/standards
  general discussion, 25–29
  vetting valuators, 31–32
Crowder v. Crowder, 44, 51–52, 165
current earnings method, 104
current ratios, 73
CVA (Certified Valuation Analyst), 28

D
"dashboard accounting method," 3,
  79–80
databases, 143–144, 145, 146f, 147
DCF method. *See* discounted cash flow
  method
debt, 10, 13, 89–90. *See also*
  investments
debt to equity ratios, 74
deferred tax asset/liability, 90
depreciation, 87, 122–123, 128
detailed valuation reports, 23, 55, 62–
  63. *See also* reports
discounted cash flow (DCF) method
  considerations when choosing,
    99–100
  general discussion, 10, 22
  income approach, 112–115, 115f
discounted future earnings method, 10,
  15
discount for lack of voting rights, 10, 19
discount from net asset value, 161–162,
  162f
discount rate
  calculating, 135–140
  capitalized cash flow/earnings
    method, 110–112
  common errors, 183–185
  foundational questions, 34
  general discussion, 10, 131–133
  risk and, 133–135

valuation formula, 95–97, 98, 131
WACC, 19, 139–140
discounts, 34, 43–44, 51–52
discounts for lack of control (DLOC)
    definitions and terminology, 155–
      157, 156n
    difficulties with, 151–155, 152f,
      153n
    examples, 157–158
    FMV and, 37
    general discussion, 10, 22–23, 27,
      170
    key person discounts and, 168–169
    levels of value spectrum, 152–155,
      153f, 153n
    non-additive nature, 169, 170f
    statutory variation, 43–44
    tools for estimating, 159–162, 159f,
      161f, 162f
discounts for lack of marketability
  (DLOM)
    applicability to controlling interests,
      166–168
    definitions and terminology, 162–
      163
    difficulties with, 151–155, 152f,
      153n, 162
    example, 163–164, 164n
    factors when determining, 164
    FMV and, 37
    general discussion, 3–4, 10, 22–23,
      27
    key person discounts and, 168–169
    levels of value spectrum, 152–155,
      153f, 153n
    non-additive nature, 169, 170, 170f
    North Carolina case law, 164, 165,
      168
    statutory variation, 43–44
    tools for estimating, 165–166
discretionary adjustments, 120–121
discretionary cash flow, 9
divorce, 1–2, 50–51
DLOC. See discounts for lack of control
DLOM. See discounts for lack of
  marketability

DoneDeals Comps database, 144
double dipping concept, 125–126

E

earnings model, 100–101
EBIT (earnings before interest and
  taxes), 148
EBITDA (earnings before interest, taxes,
  depreciation, and amortization), 148
economic benefits, 10
economic environment analysis, 76–77
economic life, 11
economic risk, 134
Einstein, Albert, 56, 67
Employee Retention Credit (ERC),
  124–125
Employee Stock Ownership Plan
  (ESOP) valuations, 27, 61–62
engagements. See calculation
  engagements; reports; valuation
  engagements
enterprise goodwill, 27, 45–46, 53
equipment/furniture, 87
equitable distribution, 27, 55, 61–62
equity, 8, 11, 13, 135, 184. See also
  intangible assets
ERC (Employee Retention Credit),
  124–125
errors
    in analyses, 78
    benefit stream, 182–183
    capitalization/discount rate, 183–185
    general discussion, 181–182
    income approach, 98–99
    market approach, 186–187
    normalization adjustments, 183
    pre-tax/after-tax benefits, 97
    reconciliation of values/approaches,
      185–186
ESOP (Employee Stock Ownership
  Plan) valuations, 27, 61–62
estate tax valuations
    calculation/valuation engagements,
      61–62
    general discussion, 55
    IRS Revenue Ruling, 115–116

value in exchange, 43
exception provisions, 30–31, 64–67
excess assets, 173–174, 174*f*
excess earnings method
  considerations when choosing,
    99–100
  general discussion, 11, 22
  income approach, 115–118, 117*f*
expected inflation, 95–97
expenses for benefit of related
  companies, 120

F

fair market value (FMV)
  definitions, 36–40
  fair value vs., 36, 38–39
  general discussion, 11–12, 35
  non-operating assets, 172–173, 174*f*
  North Carolina case law, 48–49, 165
  willing buyer/seller concept, 31, 36,
    44, 49
fairness opinion, 12
fair value, 35, 36, 38–39
FIFO (first in, first out) inventory
  valuation, 85–86, 125
Financial Accounting Standards Board,
  38–39
financial risk, 12, 134
financial statements, 83–86, 85*f*. *See also*
  specific financial statements
Financial Valuation (Hitchner), 76
fire sale value, 37
first in, first out (FIFO) inventory
  valuation, 85–86, 125
fixed asset turnover ratios, 75
FMV. *See* fair market value
forced liquidation value, 12, 14, 15,
  42–43, 82
forensic accounting, 27
formal projection method, 106–107,
  108
formulas
  valuation formula
    advantages/disadvantages, 97–99
    discount/capitalization rates,
      131–133

overview, 95–96, 109
  WACC, 139–140
franchises, 13, 57. *See also* intangible
  assets
free cash flow. *See* net cash flow
furniture/equipment, 87

G

generally accepted accounting principles
  (GAAP), 79, 83, 85*f*, 120, 122–123
gift tax valuations, 43, 55, 61–62,
  115–116
going concern value, 12, 35–36, 41–42
goodwill value. *See also* intangible assets;
  personal goodwill
    excess earnings method, 115–116
    general discussion, 12, 13, 27
    non-asset-intensive companies, 81
    North Carolina case law, 53
gross profit margin ratios, 74
growth rate, 137–138, 185
guideline company transaction method,
  general discussion, 12, 15, 22, 143–
  144

H

Hamby v. Hamby, 47–50, 169
historical financial statements. *See also*
  normalization adjustments
    adjusting, 80, 82–84
    current earnings method, 104
    excess assets, 173–174, 174*f*
    formal projection method, 108
    general discussion, 77, 103–104
    income approach
      benefit stream, 103–108
      overview, 100–103
      simple average method, 104–106,
        106*f*, 112*f*
      trend line-static method, 107–108,
        108*f*, 112*f*
      weighted average method, 106–107,
        107*f*, 112*f*
Hitchner, Jim, 76, 98–99, 156, 182
holding companies, 80–81

"How to Detect and Attack a Rigged Valuation" (Hitchner), 98–99, 182

I

income approach. *See also* capitalization rate; cost of capital; discount rate; normalization adjustments
  advantages/disadvantages, 97–99
  benefit stream
    cash flow model, 101–103, 102*f*
    earnings model, 100–101
    formula, 95–97
  calculation/valuation engagements, 56–57, 61–62
  capitalized cash flow/earnings method, 99–100, 109–112
  common errors, 98–99, 182–183
  DCF method, 99–100, 112–115
  excess cash flow method, 99–100, 115–118, 117*f*
  foundational theory, 95–97
  general discussion, 12, 22, 93–94
  historical financial statements, 103–108
  levels of value spectrum, 152–155, 153*f*, 153*n*
income statement, 9, 72–75
income tax effects, 90–92
industry analysis, 76
industry risk premium, 136, 184–185
industry rule of thumb method, 144–145
inefficient companies, 81
inflation, 95–97
Institute of Business Appraisers, 7
intangible assets
  asset adjusted book value method, 88
  general discussion, 7, 13, 43–44
  goodwill, 45–46
interest-bearing debt, 13
internal quality control processes, 27
internal rate of return, 13
Internal Revenue Code (IRC), 122–123, 128
internal transaction, 22, 144
International Glossary of Business

Valuation Terms, 36, 38, 42
intrinsic value, 13, 35, 38, 39
inventory adjustments, 85–86, 125
inventory turnover ratios, 74
investments, 86–87, 172, 173
investment value, 13, 19, 35, 38. *See also* value to owner
IRS Regulations, 36, 115–116, 117*f*, 122–123, 128

J

jurisdictional exception provision, 30

K

key person discounts, 13–14, 27, 168–169

L

land/buildings, 87, 172, 173
last in, last out (LIFO) inventory valuation, 85–86, 125
leasehold improvements, 87–88
legal risk, 134
levels of value spectrum, 152–155, 153*f*, 153*n*
leverage ratios, 74
levered beta, 14
LIFO (last in, last out) inventory valuation, 85–86, 125
limited appraisal, 14
liquidation value
  asset approach, 82
  definitions, 42–44
  forced/orderly, 12, 14, 15, 16
  general discussion, 36, 41
liquidity, 14, 163–164
liquidity ratios, 73–74
long-term debt, 13, 103

M

MAFF (Master Analyst in Financial Forensics), 27, 29
majority control/interest, 14
manufacturing companies, 80–81, 98
marketability, 15. *See also* discounts for lack of marketability

marketable, minority value level, 152–155, 153*f*, 153*n*

marketable securities, 86, 173

market approach

common errors, 186–187

databases, 143–144, 145, 146*f*, 147

general discussion, 14, 22, 149–150, 150*f*

guideline company transaction method, 143–144

industry rule of thumb method, 144–145

internal transaction method, 22, 144

levels of value spectrum, 152–155, 153*f*, 153*n*

limitations, 93

market multiples, 142–143, 147–149

market capitalization, 14

market compensation data, 125–127

market multiples

general discussion, 14, 15, 16, 142–143

selecting, 147–149

market risk, 134

Master Analyst in Financial Forensics (MAFF), 27, 29

merger and acquisition method, 12, 15, 22, 55, 143–144

Mergerstat database/reports, 143, 160–161, 161*f*

MGMA (physician compensation data), 127

minority interest, 15, 81

minority value level, 152–155, 153*f*, 153*n*

miscellaneous income, 129

N

NAICS (North American Industry Classification System) code, 145, 146*f*, 147

National Association of Certified Valuators and Analysts (NACVA)

author's expert witness training, 66–67, 117–118

credentialing/standards, 7, 27–31

net book value, 15

net cash flow (NCF), 10, 11, 15, 112–115

net operating losses (NOLs), 90

net value

Crowder v. Crowder, 44, 51–52

general discussion, 16, 46–47

Hamby v. Hamby, 47–50

Poore v. Poore, 50–51

proposed definition, 53–54

Walter v. Walter, 52–53

Niculita, Alina, 136–137

NOLs (net operating losses), 90

non-asset-intensive companies, 81

non-cash expenses adjustments, 102

non-compete agreements, 81

non-marketable, minority value level, 152–155, 153*f*, 153*n*

non-operating assets, 16, 120, 172–173, 174*f*

non-operating income, 122

non-physical assets. *See* intangible assets

normalization adjustments

common areas needing

amortization, 128–129

COGS, 125

depreciation, 122–123, 128

miscellaneous income, 129

officer/reasonable compensation, 120, 125–127

personal expenses, 120, 129

rent expense, 120, 127–128

revenue, 85*f*, 123–125

common errors, 183

control/discretionary adjustments, 120–121

ERC, 124–125

foundational questions, 34

GAAP, 120, 122–123

general discussion, 16, 100, 119, 130

non-operating assets, 120

non-recurring adjustments, 120, 122, 124–125

operating assets adjustments, 120

tax basis accounting, 85*f*, 122–123

North American Industry Classification System (NAICS) code, 145, 146*f*, 147
North Carolina case law
   Crowder v. Crowder, 44, 51–52
   on DLOC, 158
   on DLOM, 164, 168
   FMV, 165
   general discussion, 46–47
   goodwill value, 45–46, 53, 169
   Hamby v. Hamby, 47–50, 169
   key person discounts, 168–169
   Poore v. Poore, 50–51
   proposed definition, 53–54
   Walter v. Walter, 52–53

O
officer/reasonable compensation, 3, 120, 125–127
operating assets adjustments, 120
operating cash flow, 9
operating ratios, 74, 75
operating risk, 134
oral reports, 55, 62, 63–64
orderly liquidation value, 14, 16, 42–43, 82
other current liabilities, 89

P
partnership, 175–176, 177*n*
Partnership Profiles, 162
pass-through entity (PTE) premium, 175–177, 177*n*
patents, 13. *See also* intangible assets
Paycheck Protection Program (PPP) loans, 122, 124–125
personal expenses, 120, 129
personal goodwill
   case law, 45–46, 53, 169
   enterprise vs., 27, 45–46
   excess earnings method, 115–116
   key person discounts and, 168–169
   statutory variation, 43–44
physical assets, 18
physician practices, 81, 84–85, 85*f*, 127
Poore v. Poore, 45–46, 50–51, 158
poorly operated companies, 81

portfolio discount, 16
PPP (Paycheck Protection Program) loans, 122, 124–125
Pratt, Shannon
   on company specific premium, 136–137
   on DLOC, 156–157
   on DLOM, 163, 167–168
   general discussion, 1, 5–6
   on liquidation value, 42–43
pre-engagement planning, 66, 67–68
pre-IPO studies, 165, 166
premise of value
   discounts, 43–44, 46
   foundational importance, 33–35
   general discussion, 16, 21–22, 54
   going concern value, 35–36, 41–42
   intangible assets, 43–46
   liquidation value, 36, 41, 42–44
   North Carolina case law
      Crowder v. Crowder, 44, 51–52
      Hamby v. Hamby, 47–50
      Poore v. Poore, 50–51
      Walter v. Walter, 52–53
   proposed definition, 53–54
   statutory variation, 34, 43–44
premium, 154–155. *See also specific kinds of premiums*
pre-tax benefits, 97
price/earnings multiple, 16
price to discretionary earnings (SDE), 148
price to EBIT (earnings before interest and taxes), 148
price to EBITDA (earnings before interest, taxes, depreciation, and amortization), 148
price to gross profit, 148
price to revenue multiple, 147
profit and loss statement
   cash flow model, 101–103, 102*f*
   earnings model, 100–101
   historical financial statements, 103–108
   normalization adjustments, 100, 101*f*
   valuation formula, 95–97

PTE (pass-through entity) premium, 175–177, 177*n*

Q

Qualified Business Income Deduction, 177*n*
quick ratios, 74

R

rate of return
    common errors, 182–183
    general discussion, 13, 17, 131–132
    risk and, 133–135
    valuation formula, 95–97, 98, 131
ratio analysis, 72–75
RCReports (Reasonable Compensation Reports), 127
real estate, 27, 87, 172, 173
Real Estate Investment Trust (REIT), 162
reasonable compensation, 3, 120, 125–127
Reasonable Compensation Reports (RCReports), 127
reconciliation of values/approaches, 174–175, 185–186
redundant assets, 16. *See also* non-operating assets
regulatory risk, 134
REIT (Real Estate Investment Trust), 162
rent expense adjustments, 120, 127–128
reports
    exception provision, 30–31, 64–67
    general discussion, 17, 23, 30
    identifying standards, 31
    oral, 55, 62, 63–64
    written, 62–63
required rate of return, 17
residual value, 17, 114–115
restaurant grants, 124–125
restricted stock studies, 165–166
return on invested capital, 17
revenue, 84–85, 85*f*, 123–125
risk
    analysis, 69–70

general discussion, 12
industry risk premium, 136, 184–185
rate of return and, 133–135
systematic/unsystematic, 8, 18
valuation formula, 95–97, 98
risk-free rate, 11, 17, 135
Risk Management Association (RMA), 127
risk premium, 17
rules of thumb, 17, 144–145

S

safe rate, 11, 17, 135
S-corporation, 175–176, 177*n*
SDE (price to discretionary earnings), 148
securities, 13, 14, 86, 142, 161, 173. *See also* intangible assets
service businesses, 81, 98
Shannon, Donald S., 176
shareholder loans, 88–89
Shareholder's Equity, 15
SIC (Standard Industrial Classification) code, 145, 146*f*, 147
simple average method, 104–106, 106*f*, 112*f*
size premium, 135–136, 184
special interest purchasers, 18
SSVS. *See* Statements on Standards for Valuation Services
Standard Industrial Classification (SIC) code, 145, 146*f*, 147
standards/credentials
    general discussion, 25–29
    vetting valuators, 31–32
standards of value
    general discussion, 18, 21–22
    North Carolina case law
        Crowder v. Crowder, 44, 51–52
        Hamby v. Hamby, 47–50
        Poore v. Poore, 50–51
        Walter v. Walter, 52–53
    primary
        fair value, 35, 36, 38–39
        intrinsic value, 13, 35, 38, 39

investment value, 19, 35, 38
overview, 33, 40, 41
statutory variation, 34, 39
proposed definition, 53–54
Standards of Value (Fishman, Pratt, &
Morrison), 40, 46
Statements on Standards for Valuation
Services (SSVS)
general discussion, 29–31
on reports
expression of results, 58–61
reporting exception provision,
64–67
report types, 62–63
on subsequent events, 177–178
state statutes, 27, 34, 39, 43–44. *See also*
North Carolina case law
stocks, 8
strengths, weaknesses, opportunities,
and threats (SWOT) analysis, 71–75
subsequent events, 177–178
summary reports, 23, 55, 62–63
sustaining capital reinvestment, 18
SWOT (strengths, weaknesses,
opportunities, and threats) analysis,
71–75
synergistic value, 152–155, 153*f*, 153*n*
systematic risk, 8, 18

T
tangible assets, 18
tax basis accounting
appreciation/depreciation, 87
financial statements preparation
under, 83–86, 85*f*
general discussion, 79
normalization adjustments, 85*f*, 120,
122–123
Tax Cuts and Jobs Act (TCJA), 177,
177*n*
technological risk, 134
terminal value, 17, 114–115
terminology, 7–19
trademarks, 13. *See also* intangible assets
transaction method. *See* merger and
acquisition method

Treasury Bills, 135
trend analysis, 72–75
trend line-static method, 107–108,
108*f*, 112*f*
Trugman, Gary, 163
U
ultimate value conclusion, 34
Uniform Standards of Professional
Appraisal Practice (USPAP), 29–31
unlevered beta, 18
unsystematic risk, 18
USPAP (Uniform Standards of
Professional Appraisal Practice), 29–31

V
valuation engagements
calculation
approaches, 56–57
expression of results, 58–61
overview, 61–62
scope/procedures limitations,
57–58
general discussion, 21–23, 55–56
pre-engagement planning, 66, 67–68
reports
exception provision, 30–31,
64–67
oral, 55, 62, 63–64
written, 62–63
valuation formula
advantages/disadvantages, 97–99
discount/capitalization rates, 131–
133
general discussion, 95–97, 109
valuations
common errors
analyses, 78
benefit stream, 182–183
capitalization/discount rate,
183–185
income approach, 98–99
market approach, 186–187
normalization adjustments, 183
overview, 181–182
reconciliation of values/
approaches, 185–186

tax benefits, 97
credentialing/standards, 27–32
general discussion, 1–6, 18
miscellaneous topics
  built-in gains tax on assets,
    178–179
  excess assets, 173–174, 174*f*
  non-operating assets, 172–173,
    174*f*
  overview, 171–172
  PTE premium, 175–177, 177*n*
  reconciliation of values/
    approaches, 174–175
  subsequent events, 177–178
purpose, 25–27
terminology, 7–19
value in exchange, 39–40, 41, 43
value of holder, 39–40, 41, 44, 51–52
value to owner, 13, 19. *See also*
  investments
Valuing a Business (Pratt), 1
ValuSource Market Comps database,
  143
vehicles, 172
vetting valuators, 31–32
voting control, 19
VS Section 100. *See* Statements on
  Standards for Valuation Services

W
Walter v. Walter, 52–53, 165
Wang, Shiing-wu, 176
weighted average cost of capital
  (WACC), 19, 139–140
weighted average method, 106–107,
  107*f,* 112*f*
willing buyer/seller concept
  capitalization/discount rate, 133,
    134, 139, 140
  FMV, 31, 36, 44, 49
  general discussion, 54, 121, 141, 176
working capital adjustments, 102–103
written reports
  exception provision, 30–31, 64–67
  SSVS prescriptions, 62–63

ABOUT THE AUTHOR

David E. Amiss, CPA, CVA, is a Partner with Carr, Riggs & Ingram, CPAs and Advisors, a Top 25 nationally ranked firm. With over 15 years of experience in public accounting, including business valuations, tax, accounting, and advisory services, he is responsible for valuation and litigation services for attorneys, CPAs, and their clients. A graduate of Valdosta State University, he obtained a master's degree in accounting from Georgia Southern University and is licensed as a Certified Public Accountant in North Carolina and classified as a Certified Valuation Analyst by the National Association of Certified Valuators and Analysts. A member of the North Carolina Association of Certified Public Accountants, the American Institute of Certified Public Accountants (including the Valuation Services Section), and the National Association of Certified Valuators and Analysts. He was named a National Association of Certified Valuators and Analysts 2021 40 Under 40 Honoree.

For speaking engagements, contact:

Carr, Riggs & Ingram, P.L.L.C.
6601 Six Forks Road
Suite 340
Raleigh, NC 27615
919-848-1259

To reach David directly:

damiss@cricpa.com

linkedin.com/in/davidamiss

Made in the USA
Middletown, DE
10 April 2023

28481840R00126